Driving Leaders

Lessons in high-performance leadership drawn from endurance racing

Keep Driving
Keep Leading
& Dont Crash!

Chris Cappy

Chris Cappy with Scott Good

Driving Leaders
Lessons in high-performance leadership drawn from endurance racing

Pilot Consulting Corporation
PO Box 1249
Mt. Crested Butte, CO 81225

ccappy@pilotconsulting.com
970.349.1250 office
970.349.1251 fax
www.pilotconsulting.com

Authors: Chris Cappy with Scott Good
Interior & cover design: Scott Good

Manufactured in the United States of America

1st Printing, March 2015

ISBN: 978-0-9864336-0-3

Praise from others for *Driving Leaders*

"Chris Cappy has found a powerful metaphor that almost everyone can identify with, to engage and educate those who want to lead in the 21st century. I especially appreciate his emphasis on 'seeing farther down the road,' which illuminates the importance of anticipating the future, both in driving and in business."

Joel Barker, author of *Paradigms: the business of discovering the future*

"Chris Cappy and Scott Good have leveraged the unique characteristics of automobile racing to shed new light on the practices of organizational leadership and change management. Driving Leaders *will help you get from here to there—fast!"*

Marshall Goldsmith author or editor of 34 books including the global bestsellers *MOJO* and *What Got You Here Won't Get You There.*

"I've known Chris Cappy for many years. In that time, I have seen him work in the classroom with our up-and-coming executives, and at the track trying to improve his driving skills (and help me go a little faster!). He lives the principles in Driving Leaders *every day. If you're interested in getting better in business or want to improve your driving skills, you will take something away from this book. Enjoy it and drive safely!"*

Tom Falk, Chairman and Chief Executive Officer, Kimberly-Clark Corporation

"I love the idea for the book and think the parallels are strong. I gave a TedX talk recently and I thought about using racing cars as a metaphor. I moved in another direction but thought racing held promise as a metaphor for leading these days. And, given your experience, you can talk about it directly with credibility."

Michael Canning, CEO Duke Corporate Education

"Chris Cappy offers an entertaining and useful new framework for identifying, and becoming, a successful leader."

Geoff Smart, Chairman & Founder of ghSMART, and coauthor of **Power Score: Your Formula for Leadership Success**

"*Chris Cappy and Scott Good inspire with a unique combination of coaching, storytelling, and a powerful call to action. Driving is the perfect metaphor for leading with purpose in a fast-changing world.*"

Richard Leider, international bestselling author of *The Power of Purpose, Repacking Your Bags* and *Life Reimagined*

"*As a non-car (and non-driving) enthusiast I wondered if I would be able to enjoy and learn from this book. Surprise. I found it to be an easy and provocative read that left me with a handful of ideas I could implement within my own organization. If a picture is worth a thousand words, then this metaphor is worth ten thousand. If you want to move the needle on your own leadership awareness and understand, at a deeper level, the complexities of managing change and supporting your people through difficult times, pick up this book. It's impossible to come away saying 'I knew all of that!'*"

Beverly Kaye, Founder: Career Systems International, Co-author: *Love 'Em or Lose 'Em: Getting Good People to Stay* and *Help Them Grow or Watch Them Go: Career Conversations Employees Want.*

"*Wow. Once I started I could not stop. Good job. You put hours of information into a very readable and useable book. When the book is out I will have all my management team read it.*"

Hurley Haywood, 5-time winner Daytona 24 Hours; 3-time winner 24 Hours of LeMans; Vice President, Brumos Porsche

"*In a quick and easy read,* Driving Leaders *lays out leadership concepts that I myself have applied over several businesses with great success. They are actionable, transferable, sustainable and most importantly, effective.*"

James L. Schoedinger, Founding Partner, BryteStar Capital, LLC

"*Buckle up.* Driving Leaders *is a high-speed read that gives driving for performance a whole new meaning. With endurance racing as a model for success, Chris Cappy and Scott Good succeeded in getting me to look at every-day leadership situations in entirely different ways—reminding me how valuable it is to take a fresh perspective on what you think you know. If you want to see farther down the road, drive your organization a whole lot smoother, and anticipate what's next then get behind the wheel of* Driving Leaders *and take it for a spin.*"

Jim Kouzes, coauthor of *The Leadership Challenge* and the Dean's Executive Fellow of Leadership, Leavey School of Business, Santa Clara University

"Seasoned negotiators and successful teachers know if you really want to hammer your point across, there's nothing more potent than a well-chosen metaphor. A good metaphor convinces you that the unknown is not really all that that different from the familiar; it stretches when you pull on it. Chris and Scott have pulled off more than a great metaphor; this book reaches way beyond the intersection of two apparently disparate worlds to highlight a new and exciting leadership territory. A masterpiece!"

Laurence S. Lyons PhD MSc, consultant and leadership coach, visiting academic fellow and Henley Business School, and founding author of the *Coaching for Leadership* series (Wiley).

"In Driving Leaders, *Chris Cappy provides a thrilling look inside the world of high performance driving as he translates lessons from automobile racing into insightful business advice. The book is a guide to being and doing better, whether you're driving a high performance car or leading a high performance organization."*

Jake Breeden, author of *Tipping Sacred Cows*

"Endurance auto racing and high performance driving demand the adaptation and change that leaders and organizations need to surpass current limits as our world accelerates. Building on unique insights from these pursuits, this book puts you in touch with the agile responsiveness and skills for driving change essential to stay on track as a leader. Leaders, drivers of all abilities, and anyone experiencing change will gain insights and value from this book."

David Giber, PhD, International Leadership Development Consultant

"Chris Cappy has been a friend and colleague for many years. I have been influenced by his results-based approach to consulting and education for many years. This book synthesizes real wisdom in a concise way. There is a quote in the first chapter about a champion race car driver who says: 'I can give you 90% of what any car is capable of 100% of the time.' This book is about how leaders can do that with their people. Every leader who is interested in driving the right results the right way should want to learn from this book."

Norm Smallwood, Co-Founder & Partner, The RBL Group

"The drive for executives to learn from metaphor is well established, and in these pages Cappy has captured insights from a range of racing and business sources, coupled with his own considerable expertise to shed light on change, development, and improvement. The demands of leadership have never been greater, and this little gem of a book offers insights that can benefit every business executive as they complete lap upon lap of their own endurance race."

Todd M. Warner, Vice President, BHP Billiton

"Fresh, distinctive, inspiring, and compelling. In a crowded market, with books on leadership surfacing every week, Driving Leaders *stands out by showing how the practice of performance driving can help business leaders deliver consistently-winning results. Drawing on decades of experience in both domains, Chris Cappy shows how time on the track can help leaders become more intentional and focused, keep a clear head under pressure, and build more cohesive and highly motivated teams. These are essential capabilities in today's 'chaotically fluid' business environment—Cappy's excellent phrase—as they are on the racing circuit. Highly recommended!"*

Sally Helgesen, author of *The Web of Inclusion, The Female Vision, The Female Advantage,* and *Thriving in 24/7*

"Chris Cappy will put you into the fast lane with this great read. Just after I thought all the leadership change books had been written, Chris comes up with this wonderful book. Rich in stories, anecdotes, and applicable tools that will provide answers to your tough questions as you drive change. It is a quick read with tons of metaphors connecting road racing to the rapid pace of change. You will have the benefits of Chris' ability to look through the rear view mirror on what really works when you are driving at 240 mph in your life. This book is a must to have with you for the ride."

Phil Harkins, Founder and Executive Chairman, Linkage Inc.

"Understanding and experiencing what sitting in the seat of an endurance racer requires, and understanding everything that goes into endurance racing...the preparation, the performance requirements, the unexpected changes in conditions both environmental and technical, the competition's capabilities and their responses to you, bringing the car home successfully...all of it applies to leading large, complex organizations. Frankly, the similarities are just too important to ignore. Chris brings those similarities to life in a way only he can. Anyone who leads will learn how to do it better, quicker, faster. It is as simple as that."

Paul Kirincic, Former CHRO of McKesson, and current Chairman of the Board for Marin General Hospital

"The world around us continues to accelerate. The leaders of today and tomorrow must be able to look ahead, anticipate and successfully deal with the necessity of continual change—all while already dealing with full speed transitions in their business, organizations and markets. Chris Cappy, a globally recognized leader in behavioral learning, employs real lessons from business leadership experiences and car racing to develop a relevant handbook for leaders to use to help quickly navigate the opportunities and risks ahead."

Ed Dowling, Chairman of The Board, Alacer Gold Company

"Having been close to the reinvention of companies like GE, few people know how to accelerate performance and change more than Chris Cappy. His passion for racing and organizational effectiveness combine for a compelling read."

John Izzo, Ph.D. author of *Awakening Corporate Soul* and *Stepping Up*

"Chris Cappy has provided us a gem of a book that stretches our thinking around leading and managing through strong metaphors related to high performance driving and racing. The book brings forth his invention of Challenge Based Leadership Development (CBLD) in a brilliant manner. He stimulates our thoughts through how his ex-boss Jack Welch changed the world, and Chris subsequently did the same by bringing CBLD to the world in a most impactful and powerful manner. As many of you know, Chris is one of the original founders of action learning—as he brought the learning from his GE-Welch days to the world of business. And now, he has given us a gift of his core passions which I see reigniting employees, business owners, CEOs, and executives worldwide to heighten their limits of performance, become their very best, and achieve goals beyond what anyone imagined."

Louis Carter, CEO, Best Practice Institute

Table of Contents

Dedication

Forward   John Alexander, Leadership Horizons

Preface   The Seed of an Idea

PART ONE   Performance Driving and Leadership

Chapter 1   Winning Against the Odds

Chapter 2   Beginnings on the Track

Chapter 3   The Best Drivers and Leaders

Chapter 4   Keeping Calm Under Pressure

PART TWO   Driving to Achieve Competitive Performance

Chapter 5   The Friction Circle

Chapter 6   The Learning Cycle

Chapter 7   Zones of Performance

Chapter 8   The Energy of Habit

Chapter 9   Five Fundamental Habits from Racing

PART THREE   Accelerating Change

Chapter 10   Driving Better and Faster Change

Chapter 11   Leadership

PART FOUR   Mitigating Risk

Chapter 12   Assessing Risk and Consequences

Chapter 13   Situational Awareness

Chapter 14   Pattern Recognition

Chapter 15   It's Less About You, It's More About Them, and It's Definitely About Us

Chapter 16   The Final Lap

Appendix   Everyday Driving Tips From Racing

Acknowledgments   "Pit Crew"

About the Author   Chris Cappy

About the Author   Scott Good

Endnotes

Dedication

To my wife Andrea, mother Virginia, and son AJ—my car buddies and unfailing supporters for this book and all other endeavors.

Forward / John Alexander, Leadership Horizons

THE WORLD OF BUSINESS makes generous use of metaphors drawn from the auto industry—as in *driving for results, leading in the fast lane, looking under the organization's hood*, and *leaving the competition in the dust*. But this timely, highly readable handbook goes a big step further. Author Chris Cappy, a veteran management consultant and self-professed "car guy," along with Scott Good, a serial entrepreneur and national championship-winning racing driver, contend that driving is much more than just a metaphor. Together, they argue that the act of driving—not just the thought of it, but physical act of actually *doing* of it in the right way—can teach us a great deal not only about leadership, but also about life. In this book, they literally put us in the driver's seat and show us how it's done.

The authors tune up not just *any* car as their Exhibit A, but a very fast car—one that's designed for the high-risk sport of endurance racing. Why a fast car, rather than your garden-variety Ford, VW or Chevy? Partly because it appeals to the thirst for elegant speed buried deep inside us all. You don't have to be a fan of Formula 1 racing to appreciate the exhilaration of moving fast at the controls of a finely-tuned machine. And then there's the nuts-and-bolts reality of it all. Did you know, for example, that temperatures inside a racecar's cockpit can exceed 130 degrees Fahrenheit, and that a heavily-suited driver can lose as much as ten pounds from sweat and dehydration over the course of a two- to three-hour race? I didn't.

And there's much more to it. Endurance racing at the highest levels is a sophisticated team sport, not just an isolated act of derring-do. It takes vision, planning, training, and exquisite execution by many people over a long period of time. Sound familiar? If you're a business executive, it should. High-performance leading, like racing, is emphatically a team endeavor.

Chris's and Scott's passion for this subject leaps out from every page, and it's catching. So are the keen insights they derive from their beloved racetrack—insights they demonstrate how to leverage and apply in our professional and personal lives. After all, today's business environment is nothing if not fast and furious. There's danger around every curve; if we can't learn how to see around that curve before we get there, to anticipate quickly how to respond, and then to guide ourselves and our organizations around them safely, we'll spin out of control. Isn't that what today's leadership is all about—recognizing with a clear eye the uncertainty and volatility all around us, and then coaching teams of highly-trained people to navigate through successfully? Yes, but how—how do leaders teach, align and motivate their employees to maximize business results?

To answer those questions, *Driving Leaders* escorts us into the high-pressure world of motorsports and then deftly pulls back to offer cogent advice. It guides us step-by-step through the process that leads a professional driver—or an executive—to a level of performance not previously thought possible. It's a feeling (yes, feelings and instinct in this realm trump pure knowledge) of calm focus—that relaxed state amidst chaos and confusion that nimbly guides a sports car, or an executive team, through extreme adversity. And there's more: For the ordinary, typically aimless drivers among us (myself included), Chris and Scott provide insightful pointers on how we can improve our own daily driving habits. These tips matter both for safety's sake and for attaining a higher degree of concentration and consciousness behind the wheel that can lift our performance in business and in life, too.

Finally, *Driving Leaders* blends the lessons Chris has learned from the racetrack with his own firm's vast experience working with senior executives around organizational change. Leading change is the most daunting challenge today's leaders face, but face it they must: There's no alternative. Leadership and change have become synonymous. Drawing from the example of legendary racing team owners like Roger Penske, Chris shows how to build a business case for change by involving employees and wider stakeholders in the process at every level. For the leader (or leaders—there are usually more than one), it requires a level of passion, commitment and relentless focus on results. So grip this handbook as you would the wheel and turn its pages. The ride's well worth it.

John Alexander
President, Leadership Horizons, Inc.
Former President and CEO, the Center for Creative Leadership
Greensboro, NC
January 2015

Preface/ The Seed of an Idea

THIS BOOK IS THE OUTGROWTH of a conversation I had some years ago with Hurley Haywood, the world famous endurance racer. We were meeting prior to dinner in a room filled with 28 high-level executives. The group was preparing for a competitive driving event the next morning and looking for ideas that could propel them to success.

If you don't recognize the name, Hurley is a three-time winner of the 24 Hours of Le Mans and a five-time winner of the Rolex 24 at Daytona. Few would disagree with the assertion he's one of the greatest endurance racers of all time, with an extraordinary career spanning more than four decades. He's also a bit of a personal hero of mine, so in this situation, it was a thrill to be collaborating with him as a colleague.

I had been working with the men and women in the room for some time. They were the top leaders of a Fortune 20 company that was, in turn, the dominant player in its industry. Wrestling with two strategic initiatives, they'd become mired in conflicting team dynamics along with the usual churn, spin, and politics. Stuck, and with no clear path forward, we were trying something different in an attempt to make progress. Much was at stake.

To help establish the team's sense of cohesion, to bring competing executive agendas back in line and, frankly, to compel the group into action, I'd brought them to, of all places, a road racing circuit.

My plan was to immerse the group in a performance-oriented driving experience and, at the same time, work to find a solution to their business problems. I hoped to both invite and inspire them to face the very real challenges of two quite different kinds of activities at more or less the same time.

Over the course of three days, we alternated between high-performance driving instruction and focused business discussions. These discussions revolved around ways the lessons being experienced on the track might also apply to the challenges facing the team back at the office.

On this evening, the group was preparing for the culminating on-track event, a multi-team autocross competition the next day. I'd asked Hurley to act as our world-class instructor and help set the tone for the upcoming event by answering a series of questions that helped to define his approach to winning.

When I asked to what he attributed his extraordinarily long success in racing, he said, "I can give you 90 percent of what any car is capable of, 100 percent of the time."

It was such a simple statement that I actually paused, waiting for him to say more. But that single tiny sound bite of a sentence spoke volumes about what really mattered in the life of an endurance racer; it was important to deliver a consistently great performance, lap after lap, day after day, year after year.

It occurred to me that the same is true of leaders in all areas of life. Consistently delivering winning results is incredibly important, and a critical factor in long-term success.

Someone asked, "What do you worry about most when you're driving along the Mulsanne Straight [at Le Mans] doing 240 miles per hour?" I expected an answer having to do with slower cars or debris or other dangers around the track. Instead, I was surprised to hear Hurley say, "Adrenaline. Adrenaline is the enemy."

As we discussed this in more detail, it became clear how critical he felt it was to a championship performance to remain absolutely as calm as possible, even in the middle of a *not-even-a-little-bit-calm* environment like the cockpit of a racing car rushing headlong down a dark road in the middle of the night, covering more than the length of a football field every second.

The phrase "adrenaline is the enemy" was Hurley's shorthand for the need to keep your head clear under pressure. Our bodies use the hormone adrenaline to prepare us for fight-or-flight emergencies. Triggered by fear or danger, once adrenaline begins coursing through our veins it distorts perceptions and hinders both fine motor coordination and clear thought. The result often exacerbates the problems we're already dealing with. In Hurley's case, adrenaline hindered his ability to feel, and properly react to, the nuances of the car.

The solution? Anticipation. Thinking and looking far ahead. Removing as many surprises as possible and thus reducing potential fear and/or danger. By constantly processing options, possibilities, and potential reactions to them, it's possible to significantly reduce the chance of being caught unaware by emerging events.

Hurley's practice of conscious preparation and anticipation in the middle of dynamically changing circumstances proved spot-on for the executives attending. It worked effectively both on the track and, as it turned out, in dealing with business issues, too.

It was the insight behind Hurley's answers to these and other questions, combined with the success of the approach we ended up taking, that fueled the working premise for this book. The perspectives and stories offered here come from two domains.

The first domain is my own professional experience as a business consultant, executive coach, and leader of several businesses. Over the last three decades, working in nearly 40 countries, I have both consulted and instructed in the field of change leadership. I've worked with thousands of managers and business leaders from scores of businesses in the Americas, in Europe, the Middle East, Africa, and in the Asia Pacific region.

The second domain is road racing—a domain in which I've been an avid fan for most of those years, as well as an amateur high-performance driver. I've found ways to use the disciplines of this sport to maintain focus, run consistently close to my personal best, and stay sharp in my responses to whatever challenges presented themselves.

My aim, in the pages ahead, is to offer a cross-disciplinary look at concepts fundamental to the practices of leading organizations for effective results as well as driving racing cars at championship levels. Both pursuits deal with continuous change executed at high speed, in varying conditions, often under a great deal of pressure.

What follows is intended for performance-driven leaders: those who remain open to new ideas and possibilities; those who look to learn from a broad range of experiences; and those committed to delivering their personal best every day for consistent, winning results.

My sincerest hope is that something you read here will spark a thought or new awareness that helps you do your job a little differently, or a little better, and gets you to the top of the podium in your own race, whatever that might be.

PART ONE

Performance Driving and Leadership

Chapter 1 / Winning Against the Odds

3:25 PM, January 29, 2012

ROCKETING DOWN THE BACK STRAIGHT of Daytona International Speedway at more than 200 mph, AJ Almendinger was in agonizing pain. Even as he fought to control the number 60 Ford Riley prototype, Almendinger's legs and back were cramping terribly from severe dehydration. But he was not about to give up.

No way. Not then.

Coming off a six-year streak with no major wins, Almendinger was just five minutes short of the end of one of the most grueling of all motor races, the Rolex 24 at Daytona, a 24-hour shootout of the best in the business. And *he was in the lead.*

Barely.

Finishing an almost three-hour stint at the wheel, Almendinger had held the overall lead by a small margin when, swerving to avoid a slower-class car, he'd slid wide and off the track in the first 180-degree turn. As his competitors raced down upon him, he pulled it all together and sped back out onto the track, but by then his lead had all but evaporated.

After 2,700 miles of racing, and with just five seconds separating himself from the second-place car, Almendinger had no choice but to drive flat out, despite the agonizing pain.

That he was there in the first place—in the lead, at the end of one of the world's most prestigious races—was almost as unlikely as it was that he could make it to the end without surrendering his fragile lead.

Driving for tiny upstart Michael Shank Racing, a team trying yet again to win the storied Daytona event, Almendinger was a part of a four-driver lineup that included Justin Wilson, an IndyCar driver returning for the first race since breaking his back five months earlier. It was not an all-star group of drivers.

Nor was it an all-star team.

With a fraction of the budget of much-larger competitors such as Penske and Ganassi, the Michael Shank Racing team was fighting against some of the greatest teams and drivers in the world. And yet, these down-on-their-luck and comparatively under-funded drivers now found themselves in the unlikely position of being less than five minutes away from one of the greatest upsets in modern endurance-racing history.

That is, if Almendinger could hold it all together.

Afterward, during their victory celebration, team owner Michael Shank was quoted by Fox News: "I felt like we deserved [a win], to be honest, because we've worked hard. I don't make any excuses for that. We've paid our dues for sure."

Almendinger concurred: "Right now, it's the biggest win I've ever had, because we've worked for seven years to get to this point with Mike Shank, and we've been so close so many times."

In many ways, theirs is the classic story of the underdog who makes good. But it's not a story limited to racing. That 2012 Daytona win by Michael Shank Racing is at least as much a tribute to the dogged determination and leadership skills of Mike Shank himself as it is to the skills and perseverance of his team of drivers.

This same kind of victory-against-all-odds happens every day in business, much the same as it did on the track that day at Daytona. Brutal competition, challenging conditions. They're everywhere.

Adapting to Survive

Reaching for the lead in your industry, you find that everything around you is moving at warp speed.

From behind, you're being pushed aggressively by a competitor with a technological advantage. Previously an also-ran, they recently closed the gap to the point they're now hanging on to your tail, sniffing for a way to get past.

Ahead, the industry leader is blocking all efforts to let you pull alongside. Your determination and products may be superior, but his business has market position and experience on its side, and its leaders are using every trick in the book to keep you behind.

But suddenly, conditions change. Disruptive technology or regulatory change compromises everyone's plans. Visions of the future disappear and your organization's grip on the market feels as if it's slipping. You know you need to make changes to stay on course—but what changes? And how?

How do you adapt? How do you keep the business on track while continuing to run your own race—to survive at least and, if possible, to win?

Overcoming the Challenges

For today's leader, quick reactions and adaptability in the short term are as necessary for success as endurance and sustainable performance are for the longer run.

These were the leadership challenges that first led me to look more deeply at high-performance driving—and, in particular, at endurance racing—for insights into improved performance both in the executive suite and in leadership positions in general.

While driving cars and leading organizations may at first appear to be vastly different disciplines, in truth, they're a lot more alike than you might imagine and the similarities provide surprising insight into workable approaches to the challenges of both.

As you may have already guessed, I'm a car guy. But I'm also a businessperson, leader, and consultant to some of the world's largest and most influential organizations. These include General Electric, IBM, Kimberly-Clark, Cisco, BHP Billiton (the world's largest mining company), the World Bank, and scores of others.

My love for automobiles and my *at speed* experience on tracks across the U.S. mean I see a lot of the world's challenges from a car guy's perspective. Which is to say, through the Lexan visor of a full-face racing helmet.

But while I've always loved cars, I haven't always been a high-performance driver.

Chapter 2 / Beginnings on the Track

I FIRST LEARNED TO DRIVE in the late 1960s, and my education in that regard was about the same as everyone else's. I attended a few classroom sessions before climbing into the school's beat-up trainer, then drove around town until I had enough of a skill set to pass the state test. After that, I was on my own.

Like any skill that's been learned, it wasn't long before I took my driving for granted. It got me to school, to work, and out with my friends. It gave me a certain level of freedom but, mostly, it was transportation and not a whole lot more.

Living in upstate New York, less than two hours from Watkins Glen International—one of the most legendary road racing courses in the U.S.—I managed to see some great auto racing during my formative years. As I watched, I often imagined what it would be like to be out there on the track, fighting for position, racing down the straights. But more than anything else, I thought about how fast those cars were going and how exciting it seemed. It was the speed that most held my interest, but speed in the sense of miles per hour, because that's really all I could experience from the edge of the track.

I often mimicked those imagined thrills by driving faster than I should have on the highway. However, it wasn't until many years later—as an adult— that I learned there was much more to high-performance driving than simply pressing the gas pedal closer to the floor.

Of course, by then I'd done plenty of *fast* driving—which I thought was the same thing as high-performance driving. I eventually learned, though, that zipping around the neighborhood or down the highway didn't even scratch the surface of what it was actually possible to do with a car.

Not even close.

It turns out that driving truly fast—not just in a straight line but while navigating corners, elevation changes, and a track full of other drivers striving to keep you behind—requires a totally different set of skills than those I'd developed as an everyday driver on the street.

I learned this in the mid-1990s. I'd done well enough in business and life by then to buy myself a track-modified BMW M3. On the recommendation of a friend, I attended a Skip Barber drivers' education event at Lime Rock, the famous race track in western Connecticut.

My first session on that twisting, hilly road circuit was full of surprises. With an instructor riding shotgun, I was challenged to learn the track while listening to his instructions over the noise of the car. He was pushing me toward a very different way of driving than I'd ever done before. Rather than demanding caution, he encouraged me to run at what seemed like ridiculously high speeds while expecting me to maintain control, keep my concentration, and execute his instructions. It required a highly focused level of mental and physical activity.

The emotional component was a little scary, definitely disorienting, and surprisingly exhilarating all at the same time. It certainly got my adrenaline up. I exited the track at the end of that first 20-minute session exhausted, soaked in sweat, and more than a little frustrated at my inability to process it all quickly enough. I found myself wondering if this was something I'd ever be able to do particularly well.

Fortunately, the following sessions got progressively better. I began to anticipate the course's turns and was able to put more effort into following my instructor's suggestions. My driving improved and, by mid-afternoon, I was starting to carry what seemed like fairly serious speed through some of the easier parts of the track. I was beginning to think, *I'm pretty good at this.* I may have even imagined the envy I'd generate later when I shared the details of my driving exploits with my friends over a beer.

That's when my instructor suggested I take a ride with him.

And when my world changed forever.

As people go, he was nothing special to look at. Certainly not like the handsome and vibrant racing drivers that Hollywood portrays. Instead, he looked more like a mid-level accountant. A little tired, a little pale, with thin white hair, a bald spot, and a bit of a "spare tire" around the middle.

But to say my ride with him was eye-opening doesn't even begin to do justice to what I experienced as he drove me around that storied course. He drove so hard, so fast, and yet with such subtle movements of the controls, I felt quite literally dumbfounded.

In complete contrast to his quiet demeanor and meek outward appearance, his driving was both brilliant and stunningly fast. He carried so much speed into the turns, I was sure we'd never make it through without crashing. It didn't seem possible—*a car couldn't corner like that*—but he kept doing it over and over again, lap after lap, despite my serious misgivings.

At several places on the track—places where I thought I'd really been killing it—he was so much faster that, again, I wouldn't have believed it possible if I hadn't been sitting right there beside him. In one turn, where I'd been both braking and downshifting, he drove through *without even lifting off the gas.*

It was extraordinary. This mild-mannered "accountant" with the bald spot and the paunch had confidently—almost casually—rocketed his car around the track at speeds I couldn't even imagine. It wasn't until sometime afterward that I realized I'd experienced what the late Peter Drucker once referred to as "a new dimension of performance."

That drive opened my eyes to possibilities I never even knew existed. And while what he'd demonstrated didn't seem possible, quite obviously, somehow, it was. It had happened. I was there.

Of course, being a competitive person, somewhere in the back of my head I was thinking *if he can do it, I can do it too*. I knew then that I wanted to learn how to do in my car what he had done in his, and my competitive spirit pushed me to sign up for more driving events.

I invested time, money, and effort in a quest to get better as a high-performance driver. And eventually, over time, I did. I got faster, and then faster still.

And then, faster than that.

But the lesson from that first day has always stuck with me. The idea that somewhere out there were unknown levels of performance, of possibilities well beyond what I'd been able to find or experience myself, just waiting to be realized—now *that* was a big idea.

That's what I was facing all those many years ago when I had that first glimpse of real speed, and it's what Michael Shank faced as he fought to win at Daytona despite the odds stacked against him.

"Knowing" Versus Experiencing

In my case, it was a battle against my own ideas of what was possible. After all, I thought I already knew what my car could do, and I thought I knew what *I* could do with it. Just like a business unit plugging along, blissfully unaware that it holds standards and uses methods that are less than optimal, I thought I was already closing in on the limits of possibility out there on the track.

But I was at least as woefully wrong as the manager of that underperforming business unit. And probably just as resistant. It wouldn't have been enough to tell me I could go a lot faster. I wouldn't have believed it. I already *knew* what was possible, or at least thought I did.

Not until I'd actually *experienced* that new dimension of performance—and even then, not until after I'd put long hours of thought, practice, and effort into advancing my skills—was I able to perform at anything near those levels.

Even so, I had an advantage out there on the track that the manager of that troubled business unit simply doesn't have: *Someone actually showed me what was possible.* That instructor put me in his car and quite literally demonstrated the possibilities. He *proved* it could be done by doing it himself. With that as my point of reference, I worked for years afterward to make my driving become more like his.

The Critical Ability to Change

To get better, I had to change a lot of things, some big and some little. I worked hard not only to change my driving but to understand the principles of change so I could apply them in other situations and venues.

It turns out that the ability to change—that is, the ability to both manage and drive change effectively—lies at the core of the key requirements of leadership.

From your own experience, try to think of a meaningful situation in any enterprise that doesn't require change in some form. Mergers and acquisitions? The entry or exit of a new leader? A new business strategy? Startups? Turnarounds?

The world is changing all around us and those changes, in turn, are transforming the ways we live and work. Thanks to the exponential growth of social media, intergenerational dynamics, and the emergence of ever more advanced communications technologies, organizational hierarchies are flattening. These changes are having a new and staggering impact.

In its "2013 CEO Study: Leading in Context," Duke Corporate Education painted a very different picture of the world experienced by today's corporate executives from that of just a few years ago. The report states:

"To say that the pace of change has accelerated is an understatement.

"We now live in a globally interdependent world . . . [one] that is interconnected in ways that were unheard of before and unpredictable to a degree that we haven't experienced. . . . Our current leaders must adapt and future leaders must be developed in order to succeed in this new context."[1]

Today's business environments are chaotically fluid and disruptively dynamic. Our organizations need to be ready, willing, and able to adapt at all times—to incubate new ideas, products, and services, and evolve their experiences. The organization—from the executive suite all the way down to the loading dock—needs to be ready to adapt with both speed and enthusiasm.

Because of these changes, today more than ever, it's our job as leaders to actually *lead* change, not just demand it. While an iron fist can evoke action in the short term, it's no longer a sustainable model for long-term success.

The Duke report continues:

". . . Working in an interdependent world requires the ability to truly connect with and inspire people, both internally and externally. This is both different and more challenging work than the transactional fixes of the past."[2]

Inspiration – Another Key

This emerging reality is one that begs for the qualities of true leadership; of men and women who lead by example, who inspire their colleagues and subordinates, and who create among their teams an aspiration for greatness.

It reminds me of the story of three bricklayers working side by side, constructing a wall for a new building. When asked what they were doing, the first of them grunted, "I'm laying bricks."

The second looked up and said, "I'm working to feed my family."

But the third rose from his crouch and stood proudly for a moment as he surveyed the results of their effort. With a broad sweep of his arm, he gestured to the construction going on all about them, smiled, and said, "I'm part of a team that's building a great cathedral."

Same bricks, same mortar, same project, but very different attitudes. The differences are all about perspective and passion and, as a leader, it's your job to provide both. Not only to say what's important but to demonstrate it, too, through your actions. But to do that, *you* need to know what's important.

I'm here to help with that, but I'm going to do it in a slightly unconventional manner.

Guidance From Endurance Racing

With the current rate of change in the world of business, we can't look solely at organizations of the past as models of where business is headed in the future. Of course, we can learn plenty from the historical successes and failures of other organizations, but in light of today's emerging business realities, I suggest there's a better place to look for guidance—and that's in motorsports.

The form of motorsport I think best emulates the challenges of running a business is endurance racing. After all, consider for a moment what business really is: a high-stakes team competition operating at maximum speed in ever-changing conditions under a known but changeable rule set.

Those rules come to us both in the form of regulations and societal expectations. They provide boundaries within which we're free to innovate—to use our creativity and initiative to find newer and better ways of accomplishing our goals. Often, that comes through focused teamwork. The same can be said of automobile racing in all its many forms, but it's particularly true of endurance racing.

Endurance racing comprises a relatively small part of the entire spectrum of motorsports and yet chances are fairly good that even the least car-oriented of your friends is aware of the 24 Hours of Le Mans, or possibly the Rolex 24 at Daytona.

These events represent a special kind of automobile racing and are regarded reverentially within the racing community. Stretching a full 24 hours from start to finish, they are as much about endurance as they are about racing. And that's endurance not only of the car, but also of the drivers and the team, because all are critical to success.

Endurance racing, both by definition and necessity, is a team sport that's played out under the watchful eyes of millions, but it's also very serious stuff.

It's serious first, of course, because of the potential consequences. When something goes wrong in racing, it doesn't mean a bad quarter or an unfavorable analyst's report; it means people might die.

Beyond safety, endurance racing is also serious in the business sense. At the highest levels, it requires financial, organizational, and personal commitments that parallel and often exceed those we see in the more conventional world of business.

Audi, for instance, has been remarkably successful in recent years with its efforts at the very pinnacle of endurance racing. But that success doesn't come easily. According to Marshall Pruett of *Racer* magazine, Audi's 2014 budget for their LeMans program was a cool $242 million.[3] That, to field just two or three cars at relatively few international events. Why would they—a publicly-held company with fiduciary responsibility to shareholders—spend that kind of money on something as frivolous as racing? For several reasons.

First, of course, it's for the marketing and promotional value they get as a global performance brand formed in the crucible of racing. That's a strategy that's been used successfully over the years by brands such as Porsche and Ferrari, but one that only works if you win.

And, Audi has won a lot.

But possibly more important is the mindset that comes from developing a racing-oriented culture. In 2013, Audi of America (AoA) was enjoying the fruits of a remarkable run of sales success that had brought them an incredible 92 percent improvement in U.S. sales since 2004. AoA President Scott Keogh compared the business model driving the brand's success to the culture and value of the Audi Sport racing teams.

He said, "If you race, but only race, all you've done is define a motorsports team. But if your top priority is to transfer technology and integrate the lessons from racing, then you have defined an entire company. This is why Audi races and it captures our clear view on the value of motorsports."

Continuing, he said, "Racing also provides the basis of the Audi 'challenger' culture, which is constantly looking beyond recent successes to find strategies and innovations that can keep the brand ahead of its leading luxury market rivals. It's the same approach Audi Sport uses to maintain its edge on the racetrack."[4]

So, while spending hundreds of millions of dollars on racing may sound a little crazy at first, there's a business purpose behind it for Audi, from both a marketing and cultural-transformation perspective. Through racing, the company is "building great cathedrals."

Winning LeMans or Daytona is no small feat, even for a company as large as Audi. It requires an absolutely state-of-the-art racing car, a team of world-class drivers and, behind them, a surprisingly large number of support staff. Pit crew, mechanics, engineers, spotters, strategists, truck drivers, cooks, a medical team, trainers, masseuses, hydration specialists, public relations and marketing staff, caterers, and more. Many are there at the track, while others remain back at the shop, but all are relentlessly focused on a single goal:

Winning.

Whatever it takes.

Sound a little familiar? Although the end-use offering may be different, this may seem a lot like *your* organization—or at least, how you'd like your organization to be. A dedicated team of people with a wide range of responsibilities, all working toward a common goal within a highly competitive environment and focused on achieving a winning performance.

The challenge for today's executive is to be able to successfully deal with continual change at full speed, through endless competitive transitions, while at the same time developing the skills that allow him or her to perform consistently at the highest levels. In great part, this is exactly what we look for in the best professional racers, as well.

Chapter 3 / The Best Drivers and Leaders

AS A LEADER, your role in the organization may be comparable to any (or all) of several roles on a racing team. But in some ways, it may be most accurate to think of yourself as the driver.

The Job of a Racing Driver

From outside the cockpit, racing drivers' jobs look easy. After all, they aren't running marathons or slamming into one another like football or hockey players. They work alone, cocooned and protected from all but the most grievous of incidents.

And most races don't last all that long. The Indy 500, a 500-mile race, takes only three hours to complete. That's less time than it takes you or me to drive from Cincinnati to Cleveland or, for that matter, for a pro team to play a game of football. Even during a 24-hour race, each driver's stint, or time at the wheel, is rarely longer than three hours before getting a break.

So, being the driver seems rather easy, doesn't it?

In truth, it's a lot harder than you might think and, as we'll see, what it takes to deliver a winning performance behind the wheel has parallels in driving change within your business.

Like most human endeavors performed at a high level, there's a lot more to driving a racing car than appears on the surface. Even so, it's hard to convince most people that racers should be considered athletes. They're just sitting there, after all. What's so athletic about that?

One reason it looks so easy from the outside is because it's so hard to appreciate what they're doing on the inside. Even in-car cameras don't do the driver's job much justice.

During more conventional sports, such as basketball or football, we can watch the athletes' bodies in action. There's a physical empathy of sorts available to even the most casual of fans because we can see them grimace and strain, and watch as the sweat pours from their brows. We know their level of effort *because we can see it.*

But we can't do that with racers. Racers are all covered up. They wear fireproof suits with gloves and full-face helmets. Often, they wear even more fireproof layers underneath, which insulate them all the more from our inspection and review.

The heat in the cockpit is sometimes so great it's not unusual for drivers to lose 10 pounds or more from sweat and dehydration over the course of just a single two- or three-hour race. That level of dehydration saps both strength and mental energy, both of which are badly needed because racing is very much a mental *and* a physical challenge.

For instance, Formula 1 racing cars can brake at more than *five gs*—more than five times the force of gravity —and they corner just as hard. That's about the same level of force you'd experience if you drove your car into a building at 15 miles per hour. But while your crash into the building would be devastating to the car (and maybe to you), Formula 1 racers experience these forces over and over again, lap after lap, for two or more uninterrupted hours.

Formula 1 drivers' heart rates average 170 beats per minute while they're driving and peak as high as 190. That's higher than almost any other athlete—and unlike most other sports, which tend to have spurts of effort punctuated by periods of rest, racing can last for *hours* without a break.

So, despite the fact it's being performed while sitting down, racing is highly physical.

Of course, in addition to the physical forces involved, the mental aspects are just as demanding. While the car's extreme heat and *g* forces are being withstood, the driver has to be fully engaged in jockeying for position, strategizing the next move, and dodging slower traffic. It's not enough to simply drive fast. Drivers have to be able to drive fast in heavy traffic, while both defending against and attacking the drivers around them. It's a little like playing chess while also fencing—all on the deck of a speedboat careening wildly across a roiling sea.

And yet, the fastest drivers look amazingly relaxed as they make all this happen. They need to be precise and deliberate in all their moves and quick to react to unexpected slides or twitches of the car. Their movements are subtle and smooth. Top racers can thread their way through slower traffic effortlessly, almost as if it weren't there. They seem to have a sixth sense of what the cars ahead and around them will do and an ability to react to opportunities almost before they actually appear.

Racing at the highest levels is, therefore, not just about physical prowess or cat-like reflexes; it's also about mental skills, anticipation, and the use of vision. It requires stamina, resilience, and persistence, and knowing what the race is all about. It involves effectively dealing with continuous changes and many different sorts of pressure.

Minus the fireproof suit, and hopefully without the profuse sweating and rapid heartbeat, in many ways racing is a lot like running a business at the topmost level.

Jack Welch Looks Ahead

In the 1980's, during my early career as a consultant, I witnessed firsthand an amazing feat of competitive performance in the business world. Jack Welch correctly anticipated the globalization of markets and, as a result, dramatically shook up General Electric's businesses and its management culture in his determination to get ahead of the coming wave of change.

At the time, I was working as a consultant at GE's Crotonville facility. I distinctly remember the day Welch, having just returned from a trip to the

Asia-Pacific market, stood before us both incredibly excited and agitated at the same time. He said the energy was on their side—that is, on the side of the Asians—and he knew things had to change if GE was to remain an industry leader.

That trip helped to form Welch's vision of the future of General Electric. It was the basis of his understanding of the competitive realities that lay ahead in terms of new cost opportunities and structures. It also served as the impetus behind the transformation of GE, one of the greatest business shakeups ever. Remarkably, this enormous shakeup was accomplished at a time when the company was, by almost any measure, already performing very well.

But very well wasn't good enough, because Welch understood that the game was about to change and that GE needed to change along with it. Or, really, that GE needed to change *ahead* of the game. It needed to *anticipate* the world that lay ahead and, in so doing, to get there first.

With this understanding, he used the momentum of an already successful business to aggressively challenge the status quo. He created a new model for leadership that would transform all of GE's businesses.

We called them *soft skills for a hard decade,* but thanks to both Welch's vision and his dogged determination, GE entered the '90s in an amazingly strong position. The organization had a well-focused business portfolio and an aggressive set of goals that drove extraordinary—and incredibly consistent—performance.

In racing, what separates the best drivers from all the others is the level and duration of concentration they're able to sustain. Through all the physical challenges—the extreme heat, the dehydration, and the physical and mental pressures they have to endure—the best drivers somehow manage to maintain absolute concentration and focus. In many ways, that's no different than the stamina, determination, and vision needed by Jack Welch to transform GE.

Ultimately, those qualities create winners. The greatest drivers and the greatest leaders are surprisingly similar in these ways. They've trained and prepared themselves both physically and mentally and are ready to play the parts required of them to deliver at the highest level, day in and day out.

Chapter 4

Keeping Calm Under Pressure

LOOKING BACK ON MY REACTION to that first real at-speed experience, and my surprise in discovering unknown levels of performance, I realize I should have known all along that that would happen. After all, helping people push through barriers and achieve new dimensions of performance is what my professional work has been about for more than 30 years.

My work centers around an approach to learning I call Challenge-Based Leadership Development (CBLD), which grew out of my involvement at GE. This approach combines theoretical learning with direct application to the leader-learner's most significant leadership challenges by focusing on concrete delivered results, in real time.

This form of *action learning* is not about reading prepackaged case studies describing other people's challenges and actions. Instead, it's about *your* job and *your* challenges. Not in the classroom, this learning takes place in the office, or on the shop floor, or wherever you normally perform your work.

Most of my company's work involves coaching leaders and teams to help them generate next-level results. We provide executive education based on what we know works in terms of both the toolset and mindset needed to sustainably drive and lead change.

This approach is an incredibly effective form of OJT—On the Job Training—as it provides a way to push your own real boundaries, with your own real consequences, in an environment of learning and support.

It's about helping you do your job better while, at the same time, helping you develop as a leader.

We've done literally hundreds of these engagements globally, all focused on bringing people together to help them come to their own solutions and reach their own conclusions about the best courses of action to take next. By creating an environment in which simple, consistent, and disciplined methods can be applied, we see significant numbers of people come together to drive better, faster, business results.

Alignment with company goals and the incumbent focus on business strategy of the CBLD approach has made it the greatest learning approach we've ever seen in terms of creating opportunities for the transformation of people within their own organizations.

Ironically, it was exactly that kind of work that allowed me to afford the BMW I took to that driver's school in the first place, so I should have expected the kind of breakthrough learning experience I had that day.

But I didn't.

The Staggering Lesson I Learned from My Driving Instructor

I realized later that, during that ride with my instructor, I was watching a Class A exhibition of the mastery of skills. Despite the almost unbelievable speeds and high levels of braking and cornering, whenever I glanced to my left, I saw—above all else—relaxation. Mind you, *I* wasn't even the tiniest bit relaxed—we were *way* past my comfort zone. But my instructor sat there at the wheel looking for all the world like this was just another drive to the grocery store.

Also surprising, I later realized, was that my experience contrasted so starkly with what I'd *expected* that I had trouble reconciling the differences.

Like a lot of 'car guys' from my generation, what I knew about driving fast came mostly from watching car chases in the movies. The greatest of all was probably Steve McQueen's wild "flight" through San Francisco in *Bullitt,* but *Vanishing Point, The Italian Job,* and even the various *Smokey and the*

Bandit movies offered spectacular chase scenes. What did I learn from watching all those movies and countless TV shows? That driving fast involved big lurid slides, squealing tires, and drivers with grimaced faces wrenching the wheel back and forth in a desperate attempt to keep that bucking beast of a car under control.

But this scenario wasn't even close to what I saw in real life.

More than anything else, what I saw there on the track was *calm*. While there may have been a bit of tire-squealing, there were no lurid slides. My instructor wasn't thrashing at the wheel with a panicked or desperate look. In fact, it was quite the opposite. His eyes were focused far down the track, his hands and body were poised, relaxed, and his movements surprisingly economical.

He shifted gears almost delicately, with the lightest touch of his fingertips and an unhurried but deliberate movement of the gear lever. He held the steering wheel with a relaxed grip and moved it slowly and gently. His downshifts under braking were perhaps the most amazing thing of all. Using his right foot both to brake and simultaneously blip the throttle, he matched revs perfectly as he moved down through the gearbox, making the downshifts nearly imperceptible—amazingly smooth—even though he was quite literally doing two things at once.

Or often more than two.

Because, as we flew around that track, he was also talking. Chatting, really. It was a comfortable voice—not the least bit stressed—and cheerfully pointing out things he thought I should be aware of here and there.

". . . apex this one a touch early and make sure you get the nose all the way in," he said calmly as the car slid through a perfect arc, just touching the inside edge of the track with the right front tire. He rolled into the throttle, continuing the car's four-wheel drift all the way to within an inch of the exit curbing, smoothly up-shifting in mid-slide. "It'll want to run a little wide at the exit," he noted as we rocketed up a hill toward the next turn, continuing on at full speed long past where I would have been standing on the brakes. "On the way into this next turn, be sure to hold your braking until pretty late," he said as my eyes grew larger and larger with concern. "We're going uphill here so you have to be careful not to over-slow the car." He said this just as he began braking impossibly late and unnervingly briefly, before getting right back into the throttle. "This turn leads onto a long straight, so you want to be sure to carry as much speed onto it as you can. . . ."

And so it continued. Lapping the track consistently, at extremely high speeds, he took the time to almost casually point out imperfections in the track that made useful braking markers, trees off to the side that provided good reference points over the blind crests, and so on.

His actions felt absolutely incongruent with what the car was doing—like sipping cognac and having a polite conversation in the middle of a full-on bar fight. His control inputs were executed with small, confident, even *gentle* movements of the wheel and pedals, and the car itself never jerked around. It didn't fishtail. Our slides were neat and tidy four-wheel drifts. Everything was fluid and well-controlled, yet the speed itself was just *awesomely* fast. Very efficient. Highly effective.

On the Corporate Scene

This level of performance brings to mind one of my favorite clients who, at the time, was Executive Vice President of Human Resources at IBM. Very much like my driving instructor, Tom Bouchard was the absolute model of calm under pressure. Tasked with driving IBM's turn-around involving substantial reorganization and cultural changes in the 1990s, Tom ran through endless meetings in a highly volatile and dynamic environment. Day after day, week after week, he quickly processed volumes of complex and often conflicting information, yet remained remarkably calm, present, and poised. And, more often than not, silent.

You see, Tom was one of the best listeners I've ever met. Rather than always fighting for the floor to demonstrate how smart he was, Tom sat quietly, listening carefully, to learn the things he *didn't* know. When he spoke, those with any sense listened, and listened hard, because—even in the middle of sometimes highly contentious meetings—Tom had the ability to zero in on what was truly important to keep everything moving forward. He contributed to these many meetings not by domination or power but through insight, wisdom, and his unerring ability to net out complex issues based on the understanding he gained by simply listening.

In his element, Tom demonstrated very much the same thing I saw from my driving instructor, and it's what I see in many of the most successful executives as they go about their work: relaxed concentration.

My instructor was fully engaged with the car and the track, just as the better leaders are with their organizations and people. He demonstrated remarkable skill in his application of the most basic fundamentals of driving: steering, shifting, braking, and acceleration. It wasn't *what* he was doing—after all, we do these things every day in our own cars—but the *way* he did them that made the difference. The smoothness and perfection of his movements were remarkable.

The same is true of the better boardroom and C-suite executives with whom I've worked. The best seem so relaxed as they go about their days that it makes their jobs look easy, even though they aren't. Both driving and leading well require levels of expertise that come only with time. The skills needed to deliver high-quality results consistently, lap after lap, or meeting after meeting, are the by-product of experience. Of repeatedly dealing with a broad range of situations—both successfully and unsuccessfully—to a point at which the driver or executive has a solid basis from which to anticipate and react to arising challenges.

My instructor knew both the track and his car intimately. Because of this, he could explore the subtleties of the limits of both in ways I simply couldn't. He and I were working within the same set of physical limitations, but the combination of his driving skills and his understanding of both track and car made it possible for him to almost casually do things that seemed unimaginable to me.

This is true in business, too. Limits exist to what leaders can do in business situations, but the best leaders are the ones who can operate consistently and comfortably *at* or *near* those limits much of the time. They keep their focus on what's happening around them within the context of their experience. This then helps them to maintain their grip, to keep making forward progress—productively and effectively—every day.

PART TWO

Driving to Achieve Competitive Performance

Chapter 5 / The Friction Circle

IN RACING, THE IDEA OF WHAT'S PHYSICALLY POSSIBLE—that is, the actual limits of the car as opposed to those we *think* are its limits—is often represented using a graph called a *friction* (or *traction) circle.* The friction circle represents vehicular performance in terms of the forces a racing car can generate. In other words, it's a graph of the forces of acceleration, braking, and cornering, as illustrated in Figure 1 on the next page.

Despite all the thousands of pounds of materials, technologies, and complex interacting systems that make up a car, only four small patches of rubber actually touch the road. All of the car's acceleration, cornering, and braking come from the amount of friction—that is, traction—those four patches of rubber are able to generate.

For every vehicle, no matter how high its level of performance, there's a point past which the tires will lose their grip on the road. You can only brake or turn or accelerate so hard before you've exceeded their limits and the car will begin to skid or spin or slide off the road.

The friction circle is a graphic representation of these limits. In reality, the actual amount of traction available at any point in time is dependent on a host of factors, including the vehicle, the tires, the road surface, weather conditions, and so on. That said, the diagram in Figure 1 represents fairly typical forces for a high-performance street car on dry pavement. It's a simple way of showing the approximate maximum traction available to the driver in each of the various directions.

Acceleration and braking are at opposite ends of the diagram because you can't do both together. The same goes for turning left and right.

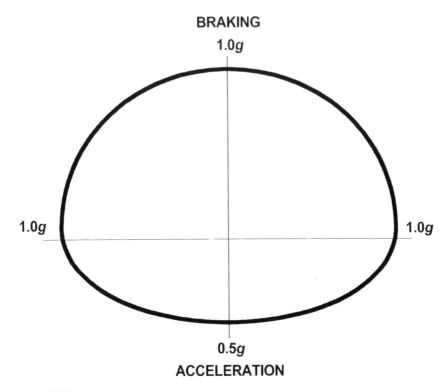

BRAKING
1.0*g*

1.0*g*

1.0*g*

0.5*g*
ACCELERATION

Figure 1. The friction—or traction—circle

The darker curved line around the outside that connects the four primary points of the diagram represents the combined limits of traction. Although the car represented by this diagram can either brake or corner at 1.0*g*, it can't be expected to be able to brake *and* corner at 1.0*g* at the same time. That would require more total friction than the tires can generate.

So, as soon as you begin turning the steering wheel, you have to give up a little braking. The more you turn, the less braking you can do, up to the point you're using 100 percent of the tires' traction for turning and can't do *any* braking, nor, for that matter, any acceleration. So, the dark circle represents the *combined* limits of traction in any given direction.

In racing, where you are being tested to deliver maximum efficiency and effectiveness, performing at or near this outer line becomes the driver's goal. At the end of a long straight, approaching a corner, a racer will first brake hard while the car is still headed in a straight line. That's what my instructor did all those many years ago. He was so close to the upper limit of traction that the rear of the car danced around slightly as the tires fought for every last ounce of grip.

That's 100 percent braking, but eventually he needed to turn. The most efficient way to do this—which is also the fastest in terms of lap times—is to begin the turn while you're still braking because that means you can wait longer to start braking. But, as we can see in the friction circle, that means you need to brake less as you turn more, to the point that eventually the car is doing no braking and all cornering.

This blending of braking into cornering while skittering around the outer limits of the friction circle is called *trail braking* because the driver is trailing off the braking as the cornering forces rise. In the second half of the corner, the opposite happens as the driver begins to accelerate onto the next straight. In that case, as he begins to accelerate, he also needs to start reducing the cornering forces by easing up on the steering wheel and, by so doing, increasing the amount of traction available for straight-line acceleration.

It's a delicate dance that lets the best drivers remain remarkably close to the outer edges of the friction circle as they navigate the endless ebbs and flows of both the track and traffic. The best racers are incredibly good at managing the transitions between braking, turning, and acceleration, and at dealing effectively with the ongoing challenges that present themselves in a more or less continuous stream.

It's important to understand that the value to racers of the idea of the friction circle is that the outer edge—the darker line on the diagram—represents 100 percent of the available performance of the car in any direction. That is, it represents the *actual performance potential* of the car, as opposed to the driver's perception of its capabilities.

The closer the driver gets to that theoretical line, the faster he'll go, but the less margin for error he'll have for correcting mistakes.

The Friction Circle in Business

But how is this useful to you as a leader in the course of transacting your business?

In business, our organizations are our cars and our friction circles are not about traction but are, instead, about the other limitations and trade-offs we have to consider. Just as the amount of available traction can vary depending on the car or the condition of the track, so may the parameters on a business-focused "friction" circle vary based on the conditions of the business.

In the car, you can't both brake and turn 100 percent at the same time. Each has to be reduced somewhat to accommodate the other. Similarly, in business, you can't spend all your money on improving production processes *and* still have more left over for sales promotions or marketing. One has to give so the other can take.

In both driving and business, it's about finding and maintaining the right balance—a balance that's constantly changing.

Figure 2 on the next page shows one possible *business friction circle,* representing the question of where you and your organization can most effectively put your focus. What are the most pressing problems you need to fix or the biggest opportunities you can take advantage of? Only so much time and money are available, so what's the optimal way to spend yours?

While we can go deep into which actions or processes should be included on the diagram, the circle itself represents a limiting factor. In driving, the limiting factor is available traction, but in business it can be all kinds of things, ranging from the availability of money or time, to legal or moral considerations. In some cases, the limiting factors may be technological access or geographic barriers.

Whatever the limiting factors are, the important ideas here are twofold. First, if you are truly dealing with a limited resource—like money or traction—you can only use as much as you have. You may be able to somehow increase the quantity available, such as adding downforce to a racing car or borrowing money from your investors, but eventually there's a limit you can't exceed. That means you have to make trade-offs as you approach that limit.

Second, is the idea that even though you have limits, often those limits are not what you believe them to be. There's no easy way to know exactly where one performance zone bleeds into the next. The dark lines in the diagrams aren't there in real life. Although very real limits exist in both business and driving, those limits have to be perceived or discovered through testing and experimentation. They have to be *learned*.

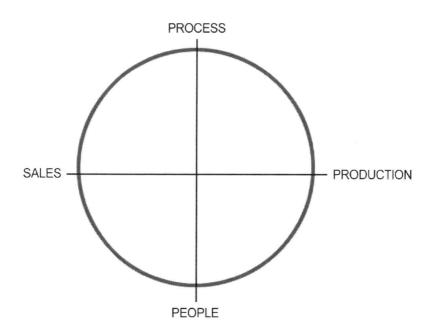

Figure 2. One possible business "friction circle" depicting trade-offs related to business

This is exactly what I was dealing with when I took that first ride with my instructor. I thought I knew the limits of my car. I was certain I was perilously close to the outer edge of my car's performance limits—until my instructor demonstrated that, in fact, I was "miles" away. It turned out I was merely close to *my* limits, which were very different from those of the car.

In that regard, my experience is pretty typical. Most street drivers have no idea what their cars can really do and, frankly, wouldn't have the skills to drive them at the limit if they tried. To achieve the outer fringes of the friction circle for more than a few seconds, you need an advanced set of driving skills. It's not enough to *want* to be able to do it; to drive consistently at the limit requires a set of skills that have to be intentionally developed over time.

In that way, driving at the limit is not all that different from occupying the executive suite. There's a reason executives have to work their way up through many years of experience before getting a shot at the top: They need that time to develop the skills required to safely control the business at a peak level of performance.

While drivers can work up to limits by gradually pushing the car and themselves harder, businesses have to find other ways to test the limits.

When I look at the most successful and most competitive of our clients, they deliberately experiment with--you might say they bet on—potential leaders by testing them with ever-new challenges and responsibilities. As a means of both accelerating and testing their skills, this process—which often involves new assignments in what sometimes seem to be unrelated areas—builds executive skills and knowledge layer by layer. This layered learning allows these leaders to be ever more effective as they move to new assignments with broader responsibilities. Although this is precisely what our CBLD process is designed to support, not everyone has the luxury of time to make it possible.

Gerstner's Challenge

When Lou Gerstner took the job as CEO of IBM, he walked into the middle of a firestorm. Over the previous few years, the company had lost tens of billions of dollars of market share and had completely missed out on the PC revolution. Prior leadership had made a strategic decision to break the company up into pieces and was paying some of its best and brightest people to become new competitors practically overnight. Its leaders were actively, if unintentionally, undermining the value created over decades by one of the most successful companies on the planet during the 20th century.

To top it off, Gerstner, the new CEO, the man tasked with turning around the largest computer-maker in the world, had no background in technology. He was hired at IBM for his brand-development and global-business acumen. From his role as CEO for RJR Nabisco and prior senior executive positions at American Express and McKinsey & Company, he had, by experience, a customer's view of IBM. However, the challenge that lay ahead required that he develop a new set of skills, that he gain a deep understanding of and appreciation for IBM's core strengths and weaknesses, and that he do it *swiftly*.

Gerstner needed to quickly push himself across performance barriers and into areas of performance where he didn't know the real limits.

Walter Irvine is the director of sales and business development for Lime Rock Park, the famed Connecticut track where I took that first ride, and he has more than 20 years of racing and instructing experience at the Skip Barber Racing School. He's had a lot of experience with people pushing through barriers.

"The problem with reaching beyond the limits we already know is [that] it involves pain," he says. "That's the whole crux of the problem. You have to push beyond your comfort zone and out to a place where you're a little unsure of yourself, where it may feel a little dangerous.

"You can think of the thresholds of learning like being the ripples in a pond. If the edge of the pond represents the limits of the friction circle and you drop a rock into the middle, there'll be a lot of concentric circles of ripples working their way out toward the edge. You can think of each of these circles as representing the different levels of personal limits.

"At the start, you're somewhere near the center, fighting limits of your own. Perceived limits, maybe, but limits nonetheless. You have to push yourself to actually get across that first ripple, but once you've done it and know it's possible, then you can go a little further, and develop your skills a little more, until you get to another ripple, the next perceived barrier, and then it starts all over again."

Over time, level by level, high-performance drivers gradually work their way closer to the limits of their cars. But it doesn't come easy, nor without constantly pushing through personal limits.

That's true not only in driving and racing, but in all facets of life.

Gerstner needed to find "the limit" at IBM, and to find it quickly. This was an enormous challenge in an organization comprised of more than 300,000 employees and tens of thousands of partnering organizations spread quite literally around the globe. He didn't have the luxury of working his way up the ladder, nor of taking the time to learn his craft, so he had to find something else. Something faster. A way to use his extremely limited time to get up to speed on the giant hydra that was IBM.

In Gerstner's case, early-on he did something surprisingly counter-cultural to get people's attention. He banned (in practice, severely limited) the use of PowerPoint presentations. Observing that IBM was drowning in beautiful and well-reasoned PowerPoint presentations that did absolutely nothing to drive action and create new value for the businesses, he once quipped that it seemed that there were some leaders there who had made their careers solely on the strength of such presentations.

Instead, he got himself up to speed by requesting white papers from all of his key executives. These documents became his means of learning about all the various businesses that constituted the company in a way he could manage in off-moments. They described the executives' businesses, their challenges, their needs, and their growth opportunities.

On Fridays, Gerstner would leave the office with a stack of white papers sometimes eight inches deep, then spend all day Saturday, and sometimes Sunday reading and marking them up. On Monday, they were returned to the executives who'd written them for clarification, extension, and expansion of their various topics. This practice typified his weekends for months. Through this simple back-and-forth mechanism, the white papers were used as a means of engaging in an ongoing, albeit disconnected, dialog from which Gerstner could quickly learn about and understand each of the company's organizations at a surprisingly intimate level. And he did this on top of his many other pressing and relentless business demands. He took his new role quite seriously.

Gerstner made it his job to listen to all of his executives. In doing so, he was not only learning about the business as a whole, he was searching for opportunities for constructive change.

Recently interviewed in the *McKinsey Quarterly*, he explained his outlook this way: "In anything other than a protected industry, longevity is the capacity to change, not to stay with what you've got. Too many companies build up an internal commitment to their existing businesses, and there's the problem: it's very, very difficult to 'eat your seed corn,' go into other activities, or radically change something fundamental about what you've been doing, like the pricing structure or distribution system. Rather than changing, they find it easier to just keep doing the same things that brought them success. They codify why they're successful. They write guidebooks. They create teaching manuals. They create whole cultures around sustaining the model. That's great until the model gets threatened by external change; then, all too often, the adjustment is discontinuous. It requires a wrench, often from an outside force. Andy Grove put it well when he said 'only the paranoid survive.'"

These white-paper dialogs helped Gerstner gain a much greater understanding of the company and, at the same time, to cultivate relationships. As a result, he positioned IBM for its historic turnaround during the first year of his tenure at IBM. Just like a driver working continuously to build skills, Gerstner put in the 'seat time' to truly learn the controls and the limits of IBM, giving him both the knowledge and ability to push it across ripple after ripple into unknown performance territory.

New Dimensions of Performance

Paul Newman was famous for being an actor, a philanthropist, and for his love and dedication to his family. Less known to many was his involvement in motorsports, where he was a deadly-serious competitor. Among the many actors who took up racing—including men like Steve McQueen, James Garner, and even Patrick Dempsey—he was likely the best. Newman grew up wanting to be an athlete but repeatedly came up short. Racing, he said, was "…the first thing that I ever found that I had any grace in."

He began his training at age 44, while preparing for a role in the classic racing film *Winning*. At an age when most racers are thinking about retirement, he quickly progressed from rank amateur to success at the professional level, amassing a record that included four SCCA national titles and a second-place finish at Le Mans. In 1995, at 70 years old, he won his class at the 24 Hours of Daytona, becoming the oldest driver ever to be a part of a winning team in a major sanctioned event.

His passion for racing led to Newman/Haas Racing, a team that fielded drivers like Mario and Michael Andretti in CART and IndyCar events, winning eight drivers' championships during his stewardship.

Newman loved the camaraderie found in the racing community and approached the challenges of the sport with a great deal with humility and humor.

He once said "One thing you learn from acting is to go out there and make mistakes. In order to do it right, you have to do it wrong, and the same is true in racing."

And, it's true in business, as well.

But, given that the role of the leader is to continuously push the organization toward newer and higher limits, how do you continue to deliver new dimensions of performance? And, how do you accomplish this while also helping those around you perform at their next highest levels—*without making fatal mistakes?*

That's a critical question in business, and it has everything to do with how we, as adults, learn new skills.

Chapter 6 / The Learning Cycle

SOME YEARS AGO, the Center for Creative Leadership took a long look at the process of adult learning and found that fully 70 percent of what we learn comes from experience. That is, from actually doing it, whatever *it* is.

To learn to do something skillfully, whether it's driving a racing car or running a business, you need seat time. Experience. But experience by itself is not enough. If that's all you have, your knowledge is limited to the things you're able to figure out for yourself. You won't get the value of next-level ideas from those who know more. You won't be able to stand on the shoulders of folks who've already been there, or who can show you a better way.

That's why the next 20 percent of what we learn typically comes from the people around us, such as a good boss or mentor. At one time or another, most of my students have had someone they worked for, they would have done almost anything for. In truth, that person is usually one of the reasons they ended up in my classes as rising leaders in the first place.

Somewhere along the way, that boss or mentor took an interest and tried to help guide their development and growth. Without his or her interest and encouragement, most wouldn't have stretched so far and probably wouldn't have moved to that next level, to that next threshold in the organization.

They grew and blossomed because that person took a chance and, first, hired or recommended them, then nurtured them along the way. Eventually, those folks made it to me, in part because they'd been given some guidance. They'd been encouraged. They'd had the right kind of 20 percent in their developmental mix.

What they had, in essence, were coaches.

The Importance of Coaches and Mentors

Even the fastest racing drivers have coaches, as do the best athletes of all kinds. And so do business executives. My friend Marshall Goldsmith was recognized in 2011 as the most influential leadership thinker in the world by *Thinkers50/Harvard Business Review*. He's also perhaps the world's most famous executive coach, having pioneered several highly effective techniques to help executives hone their craft and sharpen their skills. His research measuring the impact of follow-up with those being coached is the benchmark in the field of executive development and he contends that follow-up is the #1 difference maker in the whole change process.

At the core, his process asks simple questions of the people who work directly with and for his executive client to ascertain whether that executive performs a number of basic but critical functions. What is commonly known as the *360-degree review* is effective because, unlike most reviews, it doesn't come only from the folks higher up in the organization. Instead, it comes from the people that person actually works with, regardless of where they may be in the organization.

The goal of the 360-degree review is to answer basic questions such as:

Does the executive in question . . .

- clearly communicate a vision?
- treat people with respect?
- solicit contrary opinions?
- encourage other people's ideas?
- listen to other people in meetings?

At the root of his process is the idea that real improvement demands consistent effort and practice in an environment with appropriate support and following up to assess progress. That, Goldsmith says, is the fundamental recipe for helping people be and do better.

"Robert" – A Coaching Story

Myron Radio, one of the most experienced coaches on our Pilot team, shares a coaching story that wonderfully illustrates the value of not only the 360-degree review but also the power of executive coaching used properly.

One of our clients had a highly-experienced, highly successful sales executive we'll call Robert, but the company was having an absolutely miserable time dealing with him.

Throughout his career, Robert had always worked in the area of sales and business development, and he always hit his numbers. Always. His sales performance was quite literally at the top of the chart; but while he was excellent at dealing with customers and folks outside the organization, inside the organization, the guy was a tyrant. It was his way or the highway. He was demanding, even demeaning to the people around him. He shouted, he yelled. He screamed. He would do virtually anything to get what he wanted, the way he wanted it, when he wanted it. Disruption or discomfort to the company or others were of no concern to him. What mattered—the only thing that mattered—was whatever he thought needed to be done.

His boss finally called me and said, "We can't keep doing this. Nobody wants to work with this guy anymore. Even though he's getting tremendous results, he's killing our people internally."

So it was my job to "fix" him. One of the few tools we had was a 360-degree assessment the company had done shortly before I was brought onto the scene.

Searching for clues in that 60-plus page document, I noticed the ratings he'd been given by the folks he worked with were all over the place, but portrayed some rather consistent patterns. Some scores were quite high, some abysmally low, but two areas jumped out at me: thinking skills and interpersonal interactions.

On the thinking skills—critical thinking, strategic thinking, anything around thinking or logic—he was off the charts. Astronomically high.

But on anything related to interacting with others, he was off the charts low. Incredibly, disappointingly low.

Usually, in cases like this, we give people an additional assessment to tease out more of the underlying factors. That helps us explain the results of the 360 and refine what it's telling us—but we didn't have that luxury here.

"Just use what you have," his boss told me. "We're not wasting any more money on this."

In looking at people's skills and tendencies, everybody falls somewhere along an imaginary tasks-verses-people continuum.

In looking at his results, it was clear that Robert was way far out on the task end of the scale. So he would gladly walk into a room without any warm up, sit down, and start right into it. Let's get to it, chop chop, hurry up, faster, let's go. Not give people a chance. If they tried to explain something, he would just run them over. "I've got that. Don't worry about that," or "You don't understand what I'm telling you." That kind of stuff.

It was, as I said, his way or the highway.

And, to be fair, this was not a guy who wanted coaching. He met with me because his boss told him either he was going to change or he had to leave. Either take the coaching or hit the road.

Knowing all this, I knew I had to find a way to help Robert understand the problems he was causing. I wanted to do it in a way that would get past his aversion to coaching and let him understand the need to make substantive changes in the way he worked.

What started his turnaround was a vivid mental picture I gave him. I said, "The work you're doing is like an Olympic sport where you're getting measured on two different axes: level of difficulty and style. It's like high-diving or gymnastics, where both matter equally.

"On level of difficulty, you're getting tens all the way. A perfect ten every time. Couldn't be any better. But then there's style, and there you're only getting ones and twos. It's not a question of whether you're getting the job done. You are. Tens on that. It's about how you're getting it done. You're trampling everything and everyone in your way to make it happen.

"Imagine that in the Olympics. A ten and a two? You'd be headed home the first day and would spend the next four years working on nothing but style. Ten, twelve hours a day, six or seven days a week, you'd be working on improving your style.

53

"Well, you've got the same thing going on here. You only have half the skills you need. When you're dealing with people here at the office and getting tens and twos, you're ruining your chances for the big victory. You will never, ever, win. Not really. Oh, sure, you're going to make sales and close deals, but you'll never win the big one—you won't get the Olympic gold—because you can't. What you're doing—that is, the way you're working—is not good enough to win the gold."

He was defensive at first. He said, "Look, I don't have time for all that small talk. We've got so much to do; we've got all this work. We've got to get to it. I know what to do. If they'd only listen to me, we could get this stuff done, and we could win more accounts."

"But nobody wants to work with you," I said. "If you want to be a one-man team and do everything—all the programming, all the contracts, all the follow-up, all the legal work—if you're going to do all of that yourself, then go ahead and have at it. But I've got to tell you, you're not going to close a lot of business because you're going to be running around doing all the back office stuff that somebody else ought to be doing. You'll never have time to deal with clients. You need these people to want to work with you. When they do, you can do more—sell more—more easily because they'll have your back."

"Oh my god, I never saw it that way," he said with a shocked look as what I was saying finally sank in.

That was the start of the turnaround for Robert. From being a tyrant, he immediately toned himself down—but to the point that, after several weeks, I got another call from his boss.

"Robert's made a huge change," he told me, "but now we've got a new problem."

"What's that?" I asked.

"Now people are complaining he's being too quiet. Almost too cooperative. They need him to push more."

In his zeal for change, Robert had gone too far and overcompensated. On our next coaching call, I shared that with him.

"Yeah," he said, "people have been telling me that, too, but I'm trying really hard not to run all roughshod over them like I used to. They hated that."

"Yes, they did," I agreed. "But they want you to be who you are. This isn't about making you who you're not. We don't want to change that. We can't change that. I don't want to change what God put in. All I want to do is show you a different way of using it—in a way that's right for you and everybody else around you, too."

"You mean I can be direct with people again?" he asked.

"As long as you let them know in advance. Say, 'I need to be direct with you now.' We call it pre-framing."

"Oh yeah, we talked about that," he remembered. "I can do that."

"Exactly," I said. "Because they want you to be direct. They don't want you to be just another guy on the team who gets along. They don't want you to be soft. They need you to be hard. They just want you to be respectful while you're doing it."

So you can see from this example that while only about 20 percent of our learning comes from sources such as coaches and mentors, this learning is not of any lesser importance. In fact, given the right learning at the right time—like Robert received—it may actually be of *more* importance. It's simply a lesser percentage of what and how we learn.

The final 10 percent of adult learning comes from content delivered in some structured way. It consists of information and ideas that come from reading, from live or online classroom sessions, from theoretical or even industry association discussions. It might partly come from personal time we set aside for reflection. All in the pursuit of getting better. We can then mix these thoughts and perspectives with our own experience and advice from our mentors or coaches to come up with newer and better things to try.

These percentages—70, 20, 10—apply whether we're learning to drive a car, fly an airplane, or run a business. Discuss it all you want, but to really learn how to race, fly, or lead, *you actually have to do it.* That's why it's so important to let up-and-coming executives do something that matters—to let them take chances and make some mistakes.

How Learning Takes Place

Looking "under the hood" to further understand how learning occurs, you find a four-step cycle, as follows.

Step 1: *Do*

First, there's the actual experience. That's the seat time. Leading in the line of fire. *Doing* whatever you want to learn to get better at doing. It's about making something happen.

Step 2: *Assess*

Then there's some form of "debriefing." This process takes place after the fact and outside the heat of battle. The learner has a chance to dive into the facts of *what happened*. It gives him- or herself time to intellectually reconstruct events, to analyze everything that went on during that initial experience. The military calls this kind of process AARs—After Action Reviews—and that's a good descriptor.

Step 3: *Reflect*

The third step in the cycle is letting people have the time to reflect and generalize. Here, the learner addresses the question: *So what does it mean?* The standards of interpreting and getting to meaning are drawn liberally from life, from work, and from all of the learner's collective experiences that may apply to that particular experience.

Step 4: *Project Forward*

Lastly, but as fundamentally important as all the other parts, is transferring the knowledge gained from experience into the future. It's the point where the learner addresses the questions: *What can I take forward? What can I do differently or better the next time?*

Together, these four steps—Do, Assess, Reflect, and Project Forward—create a circle of growth and development that drives learning and change forward for the individual.

The Core Question

So, the only way to get faster on the track, or better at whatever you do, is by spending time building skills, questioning what you know, and pushing boundaries—both your own and those of the car or the organization. But if your goal is to become the best, or at least the best you can possibly be, how do you know when you've reached it? After all, the limits of our learning—like the limits of the friction circle—are invisible.

This is perhaps the core question related to any top-of-the-class endeavor. *How do you know what's possible?* In amateur racing, we often see whole classes of cars racing hard and close, thinking they're running at maximum speed—until a faster driver comes along. Then, suddenly, maybe even overnight, the whole field speeds up. Not because their cars are any different or any faster than they were the day before, but simply because somebody raised the bar and demonstrated that more was possible.

But if you're the leader, *you* have to set the bar. You're the one who has to establish what's possible, and you have to do it without crashing in the process.

Jack Welch, Stepping Up

At GE, Jack Welch did this by demonstrating a remarkable discipline to pursue new and better ways to win in business *every day*. Among his many talents, three attributes stand out as particularly critical to his success: 1) a penetrating curiosity and focus; 2) a huge intellect; and 3) his training as a chemical engineer. This last gave him both the desire and ability to go deep into any process or argument and all three, coupled with a strong Type-A competitive drive, made him a force to behold. His everyday mantra and leadership message was to *keep stepping up*. That is, to push beyond the current limits. To get past that next ripple in the pond.

These characteristics showed themselves in many ways. For instance, I distinctly recall sitting at a table in the cafeteria of GE's Crotonville global leadership center when Welch walked up to our table.

"Excuse me," he said, gesturing to the man standing next to him. "I'd like you to meet my friend Sam. This is Sam Walton."

This was the early 1990s, and Walmart was hitting the radar everywhere with the remarkable growth that was allowing it to become the retail juggernaut we see today.

Welch continued: "I was reading about the things Walmart leaders have been doing to let their people quickly understand what's happening in all of their markets across the United States. They're doing things that let them gain an advantage on the basis of understanding what they're facing competitively, and I started to wonder, how do they do that? What's the idea behind this? How could we use it in *our* businesses? So, I invited Sam over to talk to our corporate executive council today. He's here having lunch with us, and I just wanted you guys to meet him and know that we're working on these things." Then off they went.

To common 'worker-bees' like us, this was part of Welch's leadership magic. His enthusiasm was immediately infectious. And something as simple as taking the one minute it required to stop and briefly connect with our table—that in itself was quite inspirational. For the company, that initial meeting with Sam Walton resulted in a significant corporate initiative, piloted first at GE Appliances, that produced an amazingly quick market intelligence-response capability and transformed the way GE approached market forecasting. They were able to get and keep themselves ahead in terms of understanding their market dynamics during the primary selling seasons and to adjust accordingly. They knew what was happening with their competitors and what was happening on the ground, in the stores, in near real time.

All of this happened because Welch was never satisfied with the status quo. He continually pushed himself and the company to go harder, to go faster, to always strive to cross over that next ripple into that higher level of performance.

Chapter 7 / Zones of Performance

THIS PROCESS OF GROWTH, of moving from one state to the next in an effort to develop new capabilities, includes three primary zones of performance. Most of us have heard of these as being: 1) comfort, 2) stretch, and 3) panic. In the process of growing into new and better skills, we often move back and forth between all three.

The *comfort zone* is easy. It's where you are when you don't have to think about what you're doing. When you're relaxed and don't need to try very hard. It's when you're not pushing boundaries. For instance, when you're having a pleasant evening with close friends.

The *stretch zone* is when you've started to "push the envelope," that outer edge of known performance. It's when you're trying to get to that next level of ability, to cross that next ripple in an effort to get better at whatever it is you're doing.

Personally, it might be dinner with a critical client or an important presentation for a senior-level manager.

In driving, it's when you're trying to go faster than you ever have and, as a result, are pushing both the car and yourself into unfamiliar territory.

On a leadership level, it may be when you're trying to get the organization to perform at a higher level or do things in a new and better way, even though you're getting pushback from the people around you.

There's often perceived and/or real risk involved in *stretch zone* activities.

The stretch zone is a little uncomfortable, but it's only through this process of making yourself uncomfortable that you're able to move up to the next level. It's the stretch zone that gets you to constructively interact with your current limits.

But there's a third level, too, and that's the *panic zone.* That's when you've pushed the stretch zone too hard. You've offended your dinner partner or blown your chance at a promotion. In racing, it may be when the car begins to spin out of control. In business, it may be when the group of employees you've been trying to get to work differently suddenly band together and go on strike—real or figurative—as a result of your actions.

The panic zone is when you've gone too far, period. But the thing is, you can't know how far is too far without sometimes slipping over the line. That's what Paul Newman was talking about when he said, "In order to do it right, you have to do it wrong."

These three zones, comfort, stretch, and panic, are part and parcel of the same process. The things that are *stretch,* or even *panic* for you today will become *comfort* for you tomorrow. Think about when you first learned to drive. Everything was either *stretch* or *panic* at first. There were too many things to see, too many cars around you, too many places where people or cars or bicycles could jump out in front of your car . . . and yet, just a few days or weeks later, all of that became comfortable.

Panic became *stretch*, which then became *comfort.*

Of course, the reality of the process is actually a little more complicated than that, because the transitions between each of these various zones become zones of their own.

Figure 3, on the next page, illustrates the various levels of performance from *comfort* in the center, all the way out through *crash*—the worst possible outcome—on the outside.

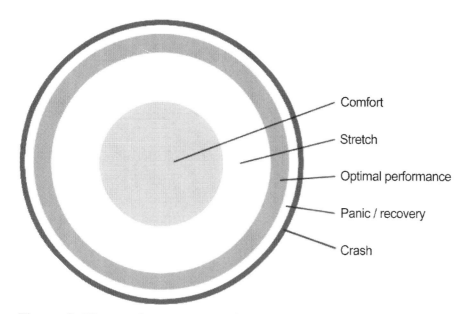

Figure 3. The performance continuum

You'll notice that both *comfort* and *stretch* are shown as relatively wide areas. Think of the width of these bands as representing margins of error. At lower levels of performance, there's still plenty of room for safely stretching your boundaries, even after you've ventured beyond the nurturing embrace of *comfort.*

The area marked *optimal performance* is actually the outer edge of *stretch.* It's here that you're getting the most from the car, the business, or yourself. Note, however, that this is a much narrower band, with a lot less margin for error. In a racing car, this is where you're working very near the outer limits of the friction circle, pushing hard toward the absolute limits of the vehicle. In this *optimal performance* area, small mistakes can have large consequences. And, the closer you get to the outer edge of this zone, the more deliberate and controlled your inputs need to be, lest you upset the delicate balance of the car or the business.

Of course, *optimal performance* isn't the end of the continuum. Beyond that is an even smaller ring called *panic/recovery.* The *panic* zone is the area between maximum performance and a full-on crash. In this zone, you either save the car or the organization or wreck it. In both driving and in life, the time you spend in *panic/recovery* is brief. Things happen quickly there, and either you make the right moves and save it, or you don't and you crash.

Pulling IBM Out of Its Panic Zone

When Lou Gerstner took the helm at IBM, the company was already immersed in the panic/recovery zone. Things were going to go one way or the other, and it was going to happen rapidly. When dealing with dramatic turnarounds, in which the straits are dire and stakes are high, the success of the initiative is almost always driven by a few key, critical decisions.

Gerstner faced monumental challenges beyond his basic need to quickly become more technologically savvy and knowledgeable about the organization. Perhaps the single most important, and at the same time delicate, set of decisions he needed to make involved who among the existing executives he should keep and who should be let go. After all, many of the folks leading the organization were the same people who had missed the opportunities and created much of the crisis IBM was then experiencing.

Although the company was in panic/recovery mode, this situation required Gerstner to deliver at an *optimal performance* level. He had little margin for error. Make too big, too radical, a change and the organization could veer badly off-course. Make too little change and it would continue to flounder. His movements—his choices—needed to be both controlled and definitive. But how do you accurately make such fine judgment calls when you're new and already over your head in the wash of details needed to learn the nuances of a business as large and complex as IBM?

I've already mentioned the white papers Gerstner requested from his subordinates. The brilliance of this move is hard to overstate. In addition to providing much-needed education in the details of the business, these papers also allowed him to directly engage leaders throughout the business in an ongoing dialog. It gave him a way to develop a sort of rapport and a more grounded opinion about the skills and capabilities of the leaders below him. From that, he could determine which of them would provide the best fit moving forward and which would have no place in the new IBM.

The net result was upheaval with stability. Gerstner managed to retain approximately half of the existing managers, who then became strong contributors to the development, the turnaround, and the value creation that came out of his leadership.

While being a superb bit of political management, the point is that Gerstner didn't arrive at Armonk that first day and just start cutting off heads. He didn't charge full speed into the turn the first time he saw it, to use a racing analogy. Rather, he studied the track and worked himself up to speed. Through thoughtful work, planning, and practice, he armed himself with both the skills and the knowledge to carry the organization back into the zone of *optimal performance.*

That's a good thing—because the alternative was bad.

That *bad* is the outer circle of the diagram, the *crash* zone, where there's no recovery. You've gone too fast or too far, and there's nothing you can do to influence events or stop what's about to happen.

Learning the Hard Way at GE Appliances

Another example of this sort of optimization involved General Electric's Appliances division in the late 1980s. The unit was one of 13 primary business units comprising GE's portfolio, but at that time, GE Appliances was what might best be characterized as a cash cow in decline.

As such, Appliances was not well-favored in the GE business portfolio. They rarely achieved GE's target double-digit growth, were plagued by global overcapacity in their industry, and hadn't seen any price appreciation for their products in several decades.

Not only were the products stagnant, but innovation was nonexistent. The organization was riddled with bureaucracy, relationships with the unions were highly contentious, and production was woefully inefficient. What success the division eked out came mostly from leveraging the strengths of the GE name and distribution system to contractors. However, it was a situation teetering dangerously on the brink of disaster which, unfortunately, eventually struck.

In a highly touted product enhancement, the company had introduced a revolutionary new rotary compressor to their refrigerator line. The new compressor was more efficient, quieter, and better in every way.

Except one.

It turned out that GE's remarkable new compressor was prone to failure in high-humidity environments that, at the time, included a significant portion of their markets. It was a fixable design flaw, but by the time it was discovered, millions of the afflicted refrigerators had already flooded the market.

Among the leadership team of GE Appliances at the time was Dave Cote, who later became the CEO of Honeywell; Larry Johnston, who became the CEO of Albertsons; Steve Bennett, who became the CEO of Intuit; and Jeff Immelt, the current CEO of GE. HR leadership included Bob Colman, who became CHRO of Delta Airlines and who was succeeded by Susan Peters, the current CHRO of GE. But at the time, they were all a part of GE Appliances and they all had a very large problem on their hands.

Not only did they have a massive recall—hundreds of millions of dollars worth—staring them in the face, but GE Appliances had no chance of producing the kind of efficiencies needed to cover the loss. If the situation were to continue as it had in the past, the cash cow would be dead.

This was GE Appliances' *panic/recovery* moment and the moves that were made in the short time available would literally decide the fate of the company.

I've often said that one of the benefits of extraordinary pain is its ability to focus your attention. Such was the case at GE Appliances. With the fate of the company and tens of thousands of jobs hanging in the balance, the new General Manager, Dick Stoneseiffer, along with the likes of Cote, Johnston, Bennett, and Immelt, quite literally transformed the organization.

They significantly reduced bureaucracy, renewed union and employee relations, kick-started innovation, and implemented production efficiencies. Thus, the company clawed its way back from the brink.

Leveraging and re-directing the massive Workout initiative then coursing through the rest of GE, the Appliances group found ways to solve not just the surface issues but also the core problems lying at the root of the company's trouble. By using the Workout problem-solving tools and deeply engaging the labor force, they were able to turn the business around and, ultimately, save the many factories and suppliers, along with the huge GE Appliance Park, from extinction.

The company had driven itself deep into the *panic/recovery* band of the performance continuum through a combination of neglect, bad habits, and problem-avoidance. Quick and decisive action by not only skilled leaders but the corporation as a whole pulled it back from the brink.

This idea of the performance continuum is powerful from a leadership point of view, and it's what racing drivers live by every day. Theirs is a constant battle to drive faster, to push a bit closer to the edge, expanding beyond their levels of comfort, out into unknown performance territory.

No leaders want to find themselves in the position of the executives at GE Appliances, but once the company or the car or the game is truly on the line, while it can be frightening, it can also be exhilarating. There is enormous energy available to be redirected in times of great challenge. How that energy is harnessed is a defining time for leadership, and smart leaders, as is sometimes said, "never waste a good crisis." In GE's case, that leadership team came together to fix the underlying core issues of that business.

And while dealing with major change and upheaval is uncomfortable, in nearly all cases, dealing with challenge or crisis effectively is, to a great extent, a matter of finding a way to become comfortable with the uncomfortable.

Chapter 8 / The Energy of Habit

IN HIS BOOK *Outliers: The Story of Success*, Malcolm Gladwell suggests that success in any field results, to a large extent, from roughly 10,000 hours of practicing tasks specific to that field.[5] That's why there's more to racing than driving fast and more to running a business than reading financial statements. Both require seat time—experience—and the scars and accolades that come along with it.

In that way, learning to race or run a business is no different than learning to tie your shoes, or write software. What starts out as foreign soon becomes familiar, and then habit, through repetition and focused attention.

Most of the things we do, whether it's how we drive, how we make a cup of coffee, or how we interact with others, are done in predictable ways. These are our habitual behaviors.

Habits are skills or actions we've wired deeply into our brains over long spans of time. As such, they are our default actions—the things we do without thinking—whether we like them or not. Repetition of any activity actually changes the way our brains function and generates an almost magical result inside our heads.

Habits Form—and Die—Hard

Charles Duhigg's number one bestseller *The Power of Habit: Why We Do What We Do in Life and Business* introduced the concept of habit into the leadership vocabulary and helped us all understand how hard it is to break even seemingly simple behaviors.[6]

It turns out that the process of repeating any action, whether good or bad, quite literally redefines the architecture of our brains. When we do something new, or something old in a new way, our brains create new links called *synapses*, which are used to remember and control that action. But synapses start out tentatively and are very weak at first. You might think of them like new muscles. They're there, but they aren't yet strong.

While muscles are strengthened through exercise, synapses are strengthened through repetition. Whenever you repeat an action regularly, the synapses used to control that action grow and form stronger bonds inside your brain. Over time, with enough repetition, using those synapses becomes easier and takes less energy, until the corresponding actions become what we call habits. That explains a lot of what's going on when we move from *panic* into *stretch*, or from *stretch* into *comfort* modes.

But just like the good habits, bad habits will become ever more established if you continue to practice them over time. That's why racers are so relentless about analyzing their practice results.

At the highest level, it's been said that it's not just practice that makes perfect, it's *perfect* practice that makes perfect. Because of this, racers want to make sure they're not only practicing, but *practicing the right things*, and that their focus is where it should be.

Personal Versus Business Habits

I was told an interesting story about challenging the forces of habit, by Domenic Pilla, President of McKesson Canada, the largest health-care distributor in that country.

Domenic is a visionary leader. In 2007, shortly after taking the reins, he launched a full review of the company's overall business strategy. During the next five years, he lead the company through an entirely new diversification strategy which allowed McKesson Canada to face the headwinds resulting from the new public drug reimbursement policy affecting their business model across Canada.

As a part of that process, I worked with Domenic's change leadership team. They were on the hook to facilitate and drive some very significant internal changes, and needed an aligned approach and some usable tools to help them effectively play their parts. In the course of that effort, Domenic told me a story about the conflict between his personal comfort with habitual behaviors—that is, his personal aversion to change—and the needs of the business, which demanded almost continual change.

When it came to his dislike of change, he said, "It's legendary among people who know me. I wear a white shirt every day. Every year for Christmas, my daughters and my wife give me colored shirts. Yellow, pink, blue, whatever. They always give me other-color dress shirts. I have a closet full of them, but I never wear anything other than white.

"Every year, we take a family vacation. I love to sail, and we've sailed together as a family for years, but every year we talk about going skiing, or hot-air ballooning, or biking, or something else. Somehow, we always end up going sailing.

"When I walk into the cafeteria here in Toronto, they see me coming and the Chicken Caesar salad is already being made. I don't have to order it. They see me coming every day, and every day my Chicken Caesar salad is served.

"So, I don't like change and I'm very comfortable with my habits. I realize that. But I also realize that resistance to change is a *personal* preference, not what's required of me to play this role, nor to lead this business I've been entrusted to lead."

He continued, "Somewhere along the way, an executive coach suggested, 'Take your watch off and put it on the other wrist.' I tried it, and it was very odd. Almost uncomfortable. I didn't like it very much.

"But even today, many years later, when I come to work, I still wear my watch on the wrong wrist. Every single day. I've never gotten used to it. You would think you'd get used to something like that, but I haven't. Why do I do it? Because I need something to remind me of my real job. I need something that takes me beyond my personal preferences so I can perform as the president of this business that's facing such an amazing amount of change.

"I choose to be a little uncomfortable, to remind myself that all of us are a little uncomfortable right now, and that it's not just about me. It's about the several thousand people, my employees, who are also dealing with these changes. It's about changes to the delivery of health-care to millions of Canadians. This little thing helps remind me of the role I play and the requirements of that role so we can continue being successful."

While this simple 'watch-trick' may seem trivial, what Domenic went on to do with his business was not. He re-positioned and strengthened McKesson Canada to remain competitive with a set of creative and adaptive responses to the sea-change of market and regulatory shifts in Canadian health care. He delivered an extraordinary leadership performance directly tied to how he used, in this case, quite literally, his time.

Domenic's story raises two questions worth asking ourselves: How am I finding ways to leverage the energy of habit and repetition to my benefit? And, given the challenges I face, which one or two habits do I want to most reinforce to support my effectiveness as a leader today?

A Fundamental Habit: Going Slow in Order to Go Fast

While it's true that most talk about racing involves speed, the truth is it's often more important to go slow than it is to go fast. At least, at times.

Practice and planning make speed possible. Very few, if any, drivers show up at the track and set a new record on their first few laps. They run dozens, even hundreds, of laps to get the difficult corners mastered and their race strategies dialed in. In the same way, great leaders prepare, develop strategies, assess the competition, and practice their skills long before they ever apply them.

As I mentioned earlier, Hurley Haywood is one of America's best known and most accomplished endurance race drivers—a three-time winner of the 24 Hours of Lemans and five-time winner of the 24 Hours of Daytona.

When it comes to improving performance, he says, "I've done this a long time. Discipline is required in terms of what you do as a driver. You're continuously analyzing the risk and the reward, thinking about the rapid pack—the cars at the front—which is not always the place you want to be."

This also relates to careers and to how you manage and conduct yourself as you're seeing and seizing opportunities. Hurley continues, "Sometimes, you want to go slow. Sometimes, you want to know what the other person is capable of before you decide to make your move, setting yourself up for better advantage or a better position in the game."

So, it's not just about going full-out 100 percent of the time. In racing, a lot of the preparation, the car setup, and even the mental condition of the drivers is about managing compromise. Says Haywood, "Everything is a trade-off. You can make [the car] turn better in the slow turns, but that may make it too hard to control in the fast ones. There are thousands of choices you can make, but what you try to do is find an appropriate balance, the best possible compromise for whatever the situation is. When it's a 24-hour race, you have to anticipate and deal with different sets of possibilities than you do in a 40-minute sprint race."

Business is the same way. There's a lot of give and take, and plenty of trade-offs. Nothing's perfect. You can't have the perfect team, you can't have the perfect equipment. There's not a perfect product or service offering, so you have to compromise.

Students new to track driving often push as hard as they can in the mistaken belief that it's only by driving super fast that they can learn to go even faster. What they don't understand is that they'll be able to go faster sooner, if they start with a little less speed and a lot more concentration on the fundamentals: on smoothness at the controls, on braking and turn-in points, and on their line through the corners. It's only after they have all these components right—and are doing them in consistently repeatable ways—that adding speed will give them the kind of powerful result they're looking for.

You often see this same go-slow-to-go-fast approach in martial arts. There, you're expected to perfect the motion of your moves before you attempt to do them quickly. The power of the punch or kick comes, in great part, as a result of using the proper technique, and you can't develop the technique if you go too fast too soon.

Whatever the challenge, you have to start with correct technique before you add speed. Speed and fluidity in motion is a direct function of mastery of the fundamentals—whether it's in driving, in jujitsu, or in leading your business. It's the reason there are different levels of racing that the drivers must advance through, just as there are different levels of management to rise through on the way to the corner office. That's the business form of going slower to go faster.

Even once you've reached the top, at times, full speed may not be the right speed. Hurley Haywood explains, "Sometimes you're holding a little bit in reserve around your pacing. That's the strategy of pacing, not letting yourself get lapped so that you're still there, in touch, when the yellow flags come out and tighten up the pack. You still want to save as much of the car as you can, because the race is going to be won during the last hour or two. That's when you see everybody's cards and what they really have left, and that's where giving up that little bit of ultimate performance pays off in terms of readiness to perform when you have to."

This same principle—being positioned and ready to perform when you have to—is a fundamental habit shared among all successful leaders. One's sense of timing is a key factor in driving business performance. I've repeatedly seen the wisest leaders enter a new situation thinking about their first 100 days as a way to deeply understand what and who they're dealing with and the challenges they're facing. Once oriented, they're much better positioned to set changes in motion and pick up the pace.

Chapter 9 / Five Fundamental Habits from Racing

THE WORLD USED TO BE SIMPLER, and maintaining our focus not so hard. When we went into meetings, we were *in* the meetings and unlikely to be distracted. Our telephones remained in our offices. Incoming mail was delivered once a day. Our computers, if we had them, ran one program at a time. Multitasking was inconvenient, so, for the most part, we didn't do it.

But that's no longer true.

Today, we're constantly connected and perpetually bombarded with information. We carry our cell phones and e-mail with us everywhere. We send and receive text messages all day and all night. The Internet provides quick and easy access to information, but it also tempts us with distraction. Hours can be lost in the blink of an eye to Facebook, Twitter, or YouTube.

Throughout the day, we're in a continuous flow of interactions with family, friends, employees, and bosses, all of whom want or need pieces of our attention. We check our e-mail compulsively, monitor social media, and do online searches even as we're conversing with others. This bombardment of information too often fragments our already fragmented attention, weakens our focus, and impedes our ability to get done the things we need to get done.

Worse, the more of it we do, the more of it we *want* to do. It's a vortex of distraction, determinedly pulling us in. And as we all know, when this becomes habitual, it costs us in terms of our effectiveness.

So, if one of the key principles of success in both business and racing is the ability to maintain focus, and if our world is conspiring to make it ever harder to focus on *anything*, what can we do about that?

That's a crucial question, and one I've been interested in for a long time: How do we un-clutter our thoughts to give ourselves the opportunity for real and prolonged concentration? How do we sustain our poise and presence to deliver consistently good results no matter what?

It's not as easy as it sounds, but it absolutely can be done with a performance-oriented mindset and a few related skills. These skills can be acquired by anyone willing to take the time to learn and practice them, to wire them in as new habits.

Which brings me back to driving.

Drawing from the collective experiences of those who contributed to this book, we've identified a number of principles and practices that will help you be more successful in your own pursuit of high performance in both driving and in business.

Be Humble in Your Approach

Trying to pretend to be something you're not while on the track can be fatal. Instructors such as Walter Irvine report that the worst students are those who show up with an exaggerated sense of their own skills. The same is true of people in business. Experienced drivers and many of the world's greatest businesspeople are notable for being humble in their approach to what they do.

In 2006, Arijit Chatterjee and Donald Hambrick published a study titled *It's All about Me: Narcissistic Chief Executive Officers and Their Effects on Company Strategy and Performance.*[7] The study found that the more narcissistic (lacking in humility) the CEO, the more likely he or she would minimize risk assessments and overestimate the potential success of initiatives—especially those that would garner extra acclaim for him- or herself.

In this regard, one can't help but think of the meteoric rise and catastrophic fall of Enron Corp. Leaders there consistently took more credit for success than they deserved and refused to take responsibility for their failures. They also lacked disciplined management practices that might have driven them to a different outcome, all because they were convinced they were "the smartest people in the room."

Keep Your Eyes Down the Road

One of the core principles of racing is the idea that the car goes where your eyes are looking. Keep your eyes focused on where you want to be—not where you are now—and the car will almost magically get you there. For the most part, the same can be said of life, too, but that's not how most drivers drive nor, for that matter, how most people choose to run their lives.

Without realizing it, the vast majority of people spend the bulk of their driving time with eyes locked just a few car lengths ahead, and live their lives with sights fixed firmly on the near-term. On today, or tomorrow, or next week. While they may glance up from time to time at a road sign, building, or stoplight, or give some quick thought to "the future," it's a temporary deviation. Almost immediately, they'll go right back to watching what's just ahead.

Drivers who don't look farther down the road than the car ahead tend to lose awareness of pretty much everything else around them because of their constant focus on that single "target." There are several problems with driving like this, but the biggest is that by not looking farther ahead, drivers leave themselves no time to react when something unexpected happens.

Walter Irvine says this helps explain why one of the most common phrases people use when describing what happened during an automobile accident is "all of a sudden."

All of a sudden, a pickup came out of nowhere and hit me.

All of a sudden, there was a huge tree lying across the road.

All of a sudden, I looked up and the whole line of cars in front of me was stopped.

"When a driver describes something as happening *all of a sudden*, chances are pretty good he simply wasn't looking far enough ahead," Irvine says. "By the time he finally realizes he needs to hit the brakes, it's already too late."

Avoid Target-Fixation

The military calls this continual focus on what's just ahead, to the exclusion of pretty much everything else, *target fixation*, and not only does this bad habit make it much harder to drive (and manage) well, it also puts you at much greater risk.

The term comes from World War II, when fighter pilots sometimes crashed into the very targets they were supposed to be strafing. In the excitement of the moment, these pilots became so singularly focused on the target that they neglected to pay attention to anything else, including their own survival.

Of course, this happens outside the cockpit, too. The real estate bubble that caused the great recession of 2008 is a recent example of target fixation on a massive scale. An environment of low interest rates, ready availability of cheap money, and a political agenda encouraging widespread, if questionable, home ownership, caused even those who should have known better not to pull back but, instead, to double down. Today, in light of the bubble that burst and the financial devastation that ensued, it all seems ridiculous, if not outright criminal. How could anyone loan money on the terms and conditions that were common at that time, we might ask?

But at the time, those who should have known better were so focused on the incredible opportunities available to make money in real estate—that is, they were so fixated on the target—that they never saw the crash coming.

Plan the Drive, Drive the Plan . . . and Be Ready to Adapt

Driving on a racetrack is, fundamentally, a simple thing. The track has a known number of curves and straights. The hills and valleys are stationary. The surface is what it is. So it should be easy to do. Business is fundamentally a simple thing, too. But then, in both cases, life intervenes.

While it may be easy to lap quickly on an empty track, racing isn't done on an empty track. It's filled with other cars you need to pass and that want to pass you. There may be debris, or oil dropped by a competitor. It may be raining. Your perfect line won't be there for you all the time—if *any* of the time—so you'll need to use your knowledge, experience, pattern recognition, and situational awareness to adapt appropriately to changing conditions.

Once You Decide, *Commit*

It's important to know what's going on around you and use that knowledge, combined with your own skill and experience, to decide the best course of action. It's important to make such decisions thoughtfully, if you can, and to adequately weigh the alternatives and potential consequences. But once you've made the decision, *commit to it.* Take it seriously. Give it your all.

Once you've decided to go for that pass through the narrowing gap, or when you've committed to a new marketing strategy, commit fully. Your own commitment breeds commitment in others, forming the foundation for a successful result. Tentative efforts rarely succeed on the track or in the boardroom.

The aforementioned are best viewed primarily as disciplines. They are proven practices that help with your drive toward better performance. In Part Three, we'll look at other powerful and proven disciplines that help you to more safely and more consistently accelerate that change results you've committed to delivering.

PART THREE
Accelerating Change

Chapter 10 / Driving Better and Faster Change

AS IT IS ON THE RACE TRACK, the capacity and ability to manage through myriad changes is a fundamental issue in every business. While any company may be able to survive for a short time in a static situation, eventually it must adapt to its markets or competition or suffer the indignity of withering on the vine. An organization's ability to transform itself is crucial to long-term viability and it's the job of leadership to see that it happens.

After all, the real job of leadership is to *lead change*. On a day-to-day basis, most organizations require little or no input from their executive levels. The organization's functions, managers, and front-line workers have their technologies, processes, procedures, and generally known methodologies to follow. That's what they do every day. It's habit. Little or no leadership is required to maintain or to manage the status quo.

But when things have to change significantly? Then nothing is the same, and nothing is easy. Change is painful. It's about getting people out of their *comfort* zone and into *stretch*, or even *panic*, when they really don't want to do that.

When change has to happen, the discomfort and pain of change has to happen, too. And that's when we need skilled leaders. That's when we need someone able to set the course and to help people understand the nature of the change. That's when we need people who are able to inspire and guide the organization through the inevitable pain so that new levels of performance can be achieved.

That's where my work has been focused for the last 30 years—on helping clients lead their organizations through changes big and small. Just as fundamental high-performance driving disciplines are proven to deliver consistently better results, so high-performance change-management disciplines can accelerate performance outcomes and help you avoid getting off track.

Change Acceleration Process (CAP)

Many of the good things that I and my company do today when supporting change have evolved from our experience with General Electric's *Change Acceleration Process* (CAP). As I mentioned earlier, during the late 1980s, GE was making huge and disruptive changes across the entire organization. CEO Jack Welch was a dynamic and visionary leader who hated bureaucracy and stagnation within the organization. When he correctly anticipated the coming globalization of markets, Welch realized the organization needed to change in some fundamental ways to be properly positioned to take advantage of the coming opportunity. The CAP program was an outgrowth of GE's *Workout* process, which significantly transformed their businesses.

For the most part, Workout involved conducting business interventions using a methodology designed to engage multiple teams of people to solve their own problems and drive empowerment deeper into the organization. Three years into the project, after more than one hundred Workout engagements, Welch convened a team to determine what people were learning from the process.

One of the key takeaways was that GE's many leaders had many ideas about how change should be implemented. While similar in concept, these ideas varied wildly in approach and were rooted in personal preference and habits. In subtle ways, we observed leaders trying to transact business while speaking as if in different languages. We further observed that the strongest leaders were often most adamant that 'their' approach was the right way, despite the fact their various ways were all different.

We recognized that the company had no consistent methodology for either understanding nor for managing change in a way that would make the dynamics of the process more consistent while achieving better results more quickly. The bet GE placed was that such a methodology could really save time and drive productivity to new levels while improving the capacity to more consistently drive better, faster execution results.

So, GE being GE, they brought together a small team of academics and consultants to first analyze the situation and then create a set of tools specifically for that purpose. The group put together a set of core processes and procedures that were then provided to the consulting faculty, of which I was a member. We were tasked with helping the Business Executive Councils bring these new tools into the field, where the academic concepts were tested under fire.

Initially, the business leaders resisted. They knew this stuff, or thought they did, and figured they didn't need to be trained in yet another Crotonville course and, to be fair, some felt the process was too academic to be of much use in the real world. So, we tweaked, adjusted, and modified. We kept some things and threw out others, until we had a truly battle-hardened and reusable process that would deliver tangible results on *any* change to which it was applied.

Perhaps the biggest insight was that the winning formula involved using fewer tools, while providing more substantial facilitation support and more direct interventions and coaching support for the senior leadership teams.

The resulting process became legendary in terms of its utilization both within GE and across GE's supplier base. More broadly, the process represents one of the greatest compilations of public domain business tools ever created because GE didn't keep it all a secret. The company shared the process.

The tools that came out of the CAP program were put together in such a way that one could effectively lead by following a set of simple but essential steps. By putting those steps together, we developed a holistic approach that addressed the most important dimensions of change—any change—by the use of a replicable and proven process.

It's hard to understate the value of the results of the CAP program. At GE, we applied CAP over six-month durations. The approach was to take an executive team with a very real and serious problem and give them six months of support, utilizing the CAP methodology and tools. Although they had support all along the way, participants would come back as a group after six months to report in detail the progress they'd made, the hurdles and barriers they'd found, and the lessons they'd learned. All of this was done in the form of presentations to the entire group, because many teams were going through the CAP process at the same time. By sharing their victories and defeats publically, everyone was able to learn from everyone else.

Challenge-Based Leadership Development

This idea of teams of people working in parallel and learning together is at the root of experiential and action learning, of which CBLD is an example.

The architecture of the process consists of three pieces. First, participants must have **a real project** they need to work on—a project that's important to the organization and for which failure has negative consequences for the participants. In other words, it has to be a project that means something.

The second part involves the leaders themselves. While working on the project, we simultaneously focus on **the personal leadership dimensions** of each leader-learner. They get feedback from leadership effectiveness surveys or 360-degree reviews and, from that feedback, learn how to more effectively work with their teams and subordinates.

Finally, we have what we call **a playbook**. At its core, the playbook includes the tools and methodologies developed and proven during the CAP process at GE. Sometimes, these are combined with other tools that especially apply to the team or the business challenges in the project being tackled.

This is a methodology by which the mechanisms and tools needed to successfully implement change can be brought to the folks who most need it. That's partly the leaders at the top, of course, but it's also the managers in the middle: the people working their way up who constitute the first line of implementation and the group from which future leaders emerge.

What Determines Success or Failure?

Think back on initiatives you've been involved with in the past. Chances are some were successful while others weren't. The question is *why?*

Some of our most interesting work during the years at GE and since then has involved studying how change efforts have progressed, in an attempt to find more consistent ways to deliver positive outcomes. We've looked at initiatives that succeeded as well as those that failed, hoping to find an easy way to understand the most important dynamics of the process of change.

While any initiative involves many interacting variables—including technological challenges, timing, skills, and mindsets required—we've found that the difference between ultimate success and failure for most initiatives repeatedly comes down to the same thing. More often than not, the *real* problem with the initiatives that fail, or those that take forever to see results, has to do with a low level of acceptance somewhere in the organization. This lack of acceptance causes chaos, churn, angst, and delay.

Out of this realization came a simple formula we used with GE's businesses—and still use today—to instantly describe what it takes to make changes work:

$$Quality \ x \ Acceptance = Excellence$$

Every change has two critical components. First, there's the *technical solution*. If you're trying to improve the way your pit crew changes tires in an effort to shorten the length of pit stops, you'll need to take a long, hard look at what they do today, then find ways to make that process a little smoother, quicker, or more efficient. That's the technical solution. It is *Quality* in the formula above.

But there's also the *organizational* or *cultural* part of the solution, and that has to do with the people affected by the change and how they behave. It's not enough to simply figure out the mechanics of a better way to accomplish the pit stop because that's just one piece of the puzzle.

In addition to the technical solution—the new technique you've developed—you also need to find a way to get the pit crew and all the other stakeholders to *accept* your new solution. You need to get the right people on board. You can do time/motion studies until you're blue in the face, but if the guys who do the work don't want to do it that way—or if their managers think it's stupid or won't let them take the time to practice your new way of working—you're wasting your time *and* alienating people in the process.

So, it's the combination of the effectiveness of both the technical *quality* of your solution along with the social *acceptance* that ultimately determines the level of success of the change.

Therefore:

$$\textit{(Quality of Technical Solution) x (Level of Acceptance by People)} =$$
$$\textit{Excellence of the Change}$$

Or, the shortened version used earlier:

$$\textit{Quality x Acceptance = Excellence}$$

It's the leader's job to gain that acceptance. If you think about quality and acceptance being rated on a scale of 1 to 10 in terms of effectiveness, you can imagine that, in some efforts, you might have terrific technical solutions that are implemented poorly.

So, new processes tossed onto the backs of your workers without any buy-in from the people who have to use them might give you results like the ones shown in Figure 4.

Quality of the technical solution	x	Level of acceptance	=	Excellence of the change
7	x	1	=	7
8	x	1.5	=	12
9	x	1.5	=	13.5
10	x	2	=	20

Figure 4. Quality x Acceptance = Excellence, example 1

Because the success formula multiplies quality times acceptance, the best possible score (10 for quality times 10 for acceptance) would be 100. But even the best technical solution in the template above only scored a 20 because the level of acceptance was so low. On a possible scale of 100, a score of 20 is dismal, and you can be sure an initiative with a score like that would be doomed to failure or, at best, very limited success.

Unfortunately, as bad as the chart above looks, based on hundreds of engagements with executive teams, I can tell you that these numbers are distressingly typical of those we encounter in our clients' own self-assessments. Little surprise, then, that companies have so much trouble implementing change!

Of course, the opposite is true, too. A highly popular change with poor technical implementation would also score poorly, as it should.

It's only when the technical solution and the level of acceptance are *both* good that you see more significant numbers in the *excellence* column, as shown in Figure 5, on the next page.

Quality of the technical solution	x	Level of acceptance	=	Excellence of the change
7	x	4	=	28
8	x	5	=	40
9	x	6	=	54
10	x	7	=	70

Figure 5. Quality x Acceptance = Excellence, example 2

This isn't exactly rocket science, but it's still critical information for you, the leader of change. Not only do you need to find a solution to the problem or challenge you're facing (the technical solution), it's *just as important* to get buy-in from the people it affects (social acceptance). Gaining acceptance isn't just nice; it's a *force multiplier*.

At the heart of the issue, *that* is what leading change is all about.

Most leaders understand how to find technical solutions. Technical solutions are comparatively easy to arrive at because, among other things, they can usually be measured. Units per hour, parts per million, whatever it is you're trying to fix, involves a measurement. You can't argue about most technical solutions because statistics usually tell the final tale.

But social solutions? Delivering consistently on gaining acceptance? These aren't so easy to measure, and getting buy-in is often a lot harder than it seems like it should be. That's because change requires getting people to climb out of their *comfort* zones, which (as we already know) they don't like to do.

Broadening Social Acceptance

Most changes affect more people than might be expected at first blush. In the example of the pit crew, for instance, it seems like any changes made to what they do would really only affect the pit crew members themselves. But, when you look at the situation more deeply, you'll discover you also need to include the drivers, crew chief, engineers, and others.

Which is pretty much par for the course. Whatever the game is you're playing, a surprising number of people have skin in it at one level or another. If you don't take the time to make sure everybody is on board from the start, you're setting yourself up for failure.

Roger Penske is one of the most successful and famous team owners in all of racing. Over many years, he has fielded teams in a dazzling number of racing series, and each of those teams, in each of those series, treats what they're doing with unparalleled levels of professionalism.

Back in the 1960s and 1970s, when racing hadn't yet become the big business it is today, it was not unusual to see "professional" teams in filthy overalls and ratty T-shirts, sporting dented and scratched cars covered in grease and layers of dirt. Back then, racing was more about what happened on the track than it was about how you dressed or how your pit area looked.

What mattered then, to most teams, was usually limited to winning, but Penske saw it a little differently. His teams were a consistent and noticeable exception. Although they did *plenty* of winning, Roger was one of the first people to recognize the value of racing as a *business*, with the potential for significant corporate sponsorship.

To have a business, it wasn't enough to *be* professional; it was also important to *look* professional. His teams always arrived at the track with clean and shiny race cars, clean uniforms, and a spotless garage. As soon as the cars and equipment were unloaded, the transporters were washed so they would sparkle while sitting there in the paddock. Even when the most hurried work was being performed on the cars, the final step was always to clean and polish before they went out on the track.

Did any of these things make the cars go faster? No. At least, not directly. But indirectly, maybe so. Certainly, it made it easier for companies to view Team Penske as a place where they should consider spending their marketing dollars. But equally, or maybe even more importantly, that professional attitude and appearance became a source of pride, and therefore of motivation, for the team itself.

The man himself will tell you it's not all about money. In a May 2013 interview with *Car and Driver* magazine, Penske, a self-made billionaire, said: "I think human capital is the whole game. It's not how much money you have or how much you can get ahold of, it's the organization. You've got to keep your people committed and focused. Success breeds success—people who are successful are motivated, they work harder, and successful companies and brands are able to attract great people.[8]

The way to keep people committed and focused is to lead them effectively, something Roger Penske demonstrates masterfully. This, then, brings us back to this idea of getting buy-in from all those affected by the change you're trying to implement.

How do you do that? What can you, as a top-performing leader, do to help deliver consistently winning performances for yourself and for the people you lead?

It helps enormously to use an established process.

As we've discussed, certain disciplines are fundamentally important to delivering consistent results. Just as in racing and driving, practicing such disciplines significantly increases the odds of a better, winning performance. We have summarized these in a chart we call the *Social Acceptance Multiplier* (Figure 6).

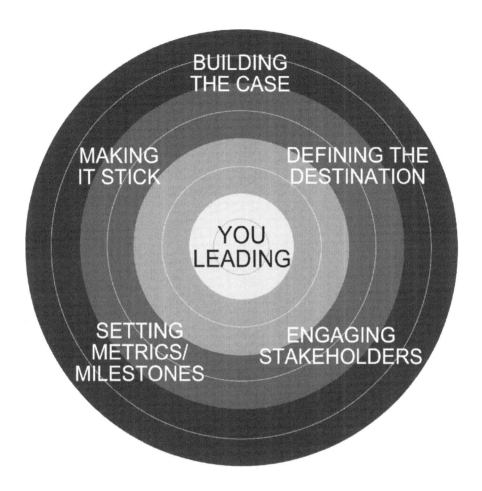

Figure 6. Pilot Consulting's Social Acceptance Multiplier

The Social Acceptance Multiplier

The process of leading the social aspects of any change can be simplified down to a few important steps: 1) building the case, 2) defining the destination, 3) engaging stakeholders, 4) setting metrics and/or milestones, and 5) making it stick. The result of successfully working through all five of these disciplines is, as the SAM chart above shows, *you leading*.

I portray these essential steps on a target, having looked at lots of targets when I was a competitive shooter. The point is that each of these are essential to keep in your field of view. Knowing where to focus and what to "shoot at" next is part of the discipline of better performers.

Of course, the devil is in the details, so let me explain each of these in a little more depth.

1. Build the case

To begin to address the social side of change, you need to build a business case that helps position the change with your various stakeholders in a way that helps them understand what's in it both for the business and for them.

You need to address questions such as:

- Why should they be interested in the change?
- What data or diagnosis exists that tells the story about why it needs to be done?
- How will the change create greater value?
- How will it change people's jobs?

Maybe it will make their work easier or more efficient, or maybe there's a raise in it for them. Maybe the change you're trying to implement will help move the organization into a leadership position in its industry and that, in turn, will mean more sales, jobs, and promotions. Maybe it will provide the opportunity to upgrade aging equipment or facilities. Or, maybe it's something else.

Regardless, you need to help the stakeholders understand why making this change is good for them *and* for the company—to engage them in addressing the fundamental question, *Why bother?* It's important to let your people be a part of the process of planning, of defining why it's important and why they should be supportive, because *that's* how you create a shared need.

2. Define the destination

This is all about answering the question, *If everything goes as planned, what will a winning performance look like?* What will everyone see, hear, and feel after this change is implemented? Use specifics. Consider the aspirational and inspirational value of what you are doing. Put the change in the context of how this helps you and your team to build that great church or cathedral. Engage your stakeholders' emotions. Make it meaningful.

Rather than say, "You guys are too slow," or "We need to work faster," you're much better off saying, "Our average output is 200 cases per hour, but our competitors are consistently hitting levels in excess of 240. We need to find a way to get ourselves over 250 cases per hour, which would make us the most efficient in the industry and the envy of all our competitors."

3. Engage the stakeholders

Who are involved, and are they in the right roles? Get your stakeholders on board, involved, and able to commit to whatever's necessary to be successful. Ask yourself, *Who are all the people this change affects?* If this is a change to a production line, certainly it will affect the folks working on the line, but there are others, too. For instance, Purchasing and Shipping. If the line moves faster, you're going to need more raw materials and, of course, you'll have more going out the door.

What about Accounting? Will the company need larger lines of credit? Will you need more, or fewer, or different, workers? That requires Human Resources. Even a small change in one part of the organization can have effects that reach deep into other areas. What about Sales? If the line starts working faster, there may be more pressure on the sales team to keep the pipeline full.

So, ironically, it's entirely conceivable you could get push-back from the sales team, the very people most likely to benefit from your more efficient production line, simply because it means *they have to change, too*. Involving and engaging people in their own problem-solving, and helping to develop their critical-thinking capabilities, is one of the keys here.

You need to consider *all of the people* who are touched by or are necessary to the changes you hope to make. Assess the impact on each of these people or groups. Is it positive or negative, and in what ways? From that, develop plans for engaging each constituency. What's their part in the process? How can you help them become a part of figuring out solutions they will own and therefore implement?

Very often, the best way to do this is to pull all the various stakeholders together to figure things out among themselves. Remember, your role is to be a guide. You don't have to know all the answers, but you do need to help them *find* the answers. Their success is at the root of your and your organization's success.

4. Set metrics and milestones

Which specific indicators can be used to track progress toward the ultimate goal? You need to find an easily understood way to help yourself and others determine if you are, indeed, making progress toward your goals. Just as drivers analyze telemetry data from laps around the track, you can use some form of metrics to determine how well you and your colleagues are doing. If yours is an effort that has concrete, measurable goals, that's great, but some initiatives have softer, more qualitative outcomes. Regardless, you need to identify milestones that can be used to measure success or failure so you and the stakeholders can review them on a regular basis, both during and after the change initiative.

5. Make the changes stick

It's one thing to implement change, but it's quite another to keep that change in place over time—that is, to lock that change in as a habit. People and organizations, both, easily fall back to more familiar ways of working. To fully embed any change into the way you do things requires implementing the change and making sure the tools, the knowledge, the skills, and any necessary infrastructure are in place to support the change moving forward.

Rewards are typically a part of this. If you tied a monetary bonus to the success of a production line's performance, does Accounting know about it? Do they know how to measure the impact of the change and when to include extra money in the team's paychecks? You can be sure the folks on the shop floor will know, and you can be equally sure that the day those bonuses don't show up correctly is also the day they begin to lose enthusiasm for "your" new way of doing things.

Does the change require any organizational restructuring or redesign? Are you able to measure the right things? Do you need to invest more in the right talent, or additional staffing? Is there a need for further training or development so the changes can be effected? Are there processes that need to be modified or improved that will enable everyone to perform at optimal level?

To lead change and to give yourself better odds of delivering the desired results, you need to consider all of these questions *early in the process*. It helps to know the kind of "heavy lifting" required to deal with the realities of your situation. Too often, these sorts of issues are never considered and end up being stumbled across much too late in the process. This affects resource calculations—the time and money actually required to get to the finish line—and often causes projects to run off track. Leaders too often underestimate the time and energy required to deliver high-performance results.

The Social Acceptance Multiplier at Work–A Review

So, to review, the point of the Social Acceptance Multiplier is to give leaders an organized way to know they're considering all the different facets of the social side of change.

The five actions in the Social Acceptance Multiplier drive social success in change initiatives. This is a time-tested, battle-proven methodology that we have used over and over again at many of the world's largest organizations with consistent and replicable success. The tools and ideas associated with each of these disciplines help executives and entrepreneurs accomplish substantive change better and faster.

But even using this tested and proven methodology won't come without a certain amount of pain. After all, introducing a new means of dealing with change is, in itself, change.

And change, as I said at the beginning of this chapter, is painful.

Which brings us back to the subject of leadership, as important as all the other five actions combined. That's why it's in the center of the bull's-eye, where the rubber hits the road. You'll read more about it in the next chapter.

Chapter 11 / Leadership

SO, WHAT IS THIS "LEADERSHIP" I keep referring to? While countless discussions of leadership exist, over the course of Pilot Consulting's 30-plus years of work, and across hundreds of consulting engagements, we have had the opportunity to ask several thousand managers and workers the question, "When you see effective leadership—that is, the sort of leader you would do almost anything for—what do you see them doing or saying?"

The results have been synthesized into four distinct behavioral qualities that cut through all the complexity and describe effective leadership. They are:

1. Seeing and seizing opportunities

2. Bringing others along with you

3. Being perceived as effective

4. Delivering results

If any of these four elements is missing, according to those surveyed, it's not leadership. For instance, there are people who are great at seeing and seizing opportunities, who deliver results, but who don't bring others along with them. This would describe a lot of sales representatives, for instance, and while they're important to the organization, they're not necessarily leaders.

Let's look at each of the four in more detail.

Seeing and Seizing Opportunities

This idea is almost self-explanatory. Core to being a leader is figuring out where the organization needs to go and what it needs to do to be the most successful. This means positioning yourself and the organization to take advantage of opportunities.

As the leader, it's up to you to make the tough decisions about which compromises need to be made. You decide which solutions provide the best chance of success moving forward and prepare your people to pounce on opportunities when they present themselves. That's what leading is all about.

So, to be effective, you not only need to recognize opportunities but also lead your company in taking advantage of them.

Bringing Others Along with You

By definition, a leader can't lead without followers. Part and parcel of an effective leadership role is inspiring others.

As you rise into the top levels of business performance, a huge percentage of your work centers on dealing with and caring for other people. You no longer have your hands directly on the controls but are necessarily working with and through other people and groups. Therefore, everything becomes a little less certain.

Running a big organization is, to a great extent, a fly-by-wire, rather than directly hands-on, situation. In other words, your movements of the controls work their way down to the folks who actually make the changes. Those movements, just like the control movements when you're driving a car, need to be done smoothly, consistently, and without upsetting the "vehicle." You do that not by forcing control, but by working with the people.

Being Perceived as Effective

This least obvious characteristic of leaders is also quite possibly the most important. It's not enough to *be* effective; to be a true leader, you must also be *perceived* as being effective by the people you are leading.

Effective leadership is a process of pulling, not pushing. The people you lead will look to you for cues to know what's important and what's not. The way you let them know the answer is through your *actions* much more than through your words.

At the heart of how you lead are five discrete kinds of actions, which we identified by asking the question: "What defined the leader you might have walked through fire for, or whom you perceived as being truly effective?"

More than your words could ever convey, the people you lead will know what is and isn't important based on the:

1. time you give;
2. energy and passion you show;
3. focus and agenda you set;
4. trade-offs of resources and talent you make; and
5. quality of relationships you create across boundaries.

We'll look at each of these actions and why they're essential for effective leadership.

Delivering Results

You have to bring home the bacon. It's what you deliver that counts. And your results will be delivered through other people.

Your job as a leader is to effect change—to make things different and, because of that difference, better. That is the *point* of leading.

However, for you as a true leader, success will not be an individual or personal effort. The choice to lead may reward you personally (and often financially), but success that comes from leadership is accomplished through and with others, not by you alone. As a leader, you are a role model. The choices you make and the skills you exhibit in leading will show in the final results of your team.

The Time You Give. The value of any change is measured by your team based on the amount of attention you, personally, devote to it. And, like all such things, what matters most is *perceived time*. That is, the amount of time the people around you *feel* you are committing to the project.

So, it's not enough to simply put in the time; you also have to create the *perception* of putting in the time. You may be working until the wee hours every night, but if your team doesn't know it, or sense it, it doesn't count toward the perception of your commitment. The value of the initiative to you—and therefore its importance—is measured by the clock *as read by others.*

The Energy and Passion You Show. As the leader, you set the tone. You need to be "turned on" by change and have a passion for what you and your team are doing, because that passion will be contagious. The mood you bring to the team is the mood they'll bring in return.

Leading change is all about finding newer and better ways of working, but it's also about showing your team the way. It's important for you to seek and support new ways of working but, more than that, you need to be a part of the process. As the inevitable roadblocks appear, maintain a mindset that finds opportunities in problems, giving your team a way to move forward rather than making excuses for why a solution can't be reached.

The Focus and Agenda You Set. The best leaders have focus—a limited set of priorities they concentrate on relentlessly. To be effective, you can't always be randomly changing paths, following the latest management fad, or arbitrarily trying new and different ways of working just to see how it feels.

Followers want to know where they're going and how they're going to get there, and they need confidence that you, as their leader, have that vision. They expect you not only to talk the talk, but also to walk the walk. To lead by example. To show them what's important through your actions.

The Trade-Offs of Resources and Talent You Make. How you allocate and handle money and people shows your commitment to the project. When managers insist on the importance of a project but then refuse to provide the necessary funding or staffing, they're silently dooming its success.

Where you commit your time and resources defines what's important to you. If a project truly matters, then it's your job as the leader to find the money and the people to make it possible. As usual, your actions in this regard speak much louder than your words.

The Quality of Relationships You Make Across Boundaries. Relationships drive results. The relationships you create working across boundaries—functional, political, and geographic—are often as important as those you maintain and nourish within your own team. Determining *which* relationships are most important to a given end is a critical skill in fulfilling your leadership agenda.

Ten Truths about Leadership

Jim Kouzes and Barry Posner, authors of the highly regarded leadership classic *The Leadership Challenge*,[9] also published a book called *The Truth about Leadership*, which pulled from a global database of more than one million participants from over 70 countries to uncover the perspectives of several generations of leaders (including X, Y, and Millennials) comprising a broad mix in terms of gender and cultural diversity.

In *The Truth about Leadership*, Kouzes and Posner present 10 truths about leadership that have stood the test of time, which they assert hold true both globally and cross-generationally.[10] These truths include the following:

1. You can make a difference. Before you lead, you have to believe you can have a positive impact on others. When you believe you can make a difference, you position yourself to hear the call to lead.

2. Credibility is the foundation of leadership. If people don't believe in you, they won't willingly follow. You must do what you say you're going to do. This means being so clear about your beliefs that you can live them every day.

3. Values drive commitment. You need to know what you believe in, because you can only fully commit to the organization or cause when there's a good fit between what you value and what the organization values. This is true, too, for the people you lead.

4. Focusing on the future sets leaders apart. You have to be forward looking; it's the quality that most differentiates leaders from individual contributors. You need to spend time reflecting on the future. Big dreams that resonate with others inspire and energize.

5. You can't do it alone. Leadership is a team sport, and you need to engage others in the cause. You need to enable others to be even better than they already are.

6. Trust is critical. To enlist others, you need to gain their trust. Build mutual trust; trust others, too.

7. Challenge is the crucible of greatness. Great achievements don't happen by maintaining the status quo. Change invariably involves challenge, and challenge tests you. It introduces you to yourself. It brings you face-to-face with your level of commitment, your grittiness, and your values. It reveals your mindset about change.

8. You either lead by example or you don't lead at all. As a leader, you have to go first. That's what it takes to get others to follow your lead.

9. The best leaders are the best learners. Learning is the master skill of leadership. To be a leader, become a fanatic about constant improvement.

10. Leadership is an affair of the heart. To be a leader, you need to love what you're doing and those you lead. Make others feel great about themselves and be gracious in showing your appreciation.

These truths should form the basis of any leadership development program. They motivate the right kinds of behaviors that form good and sustainable leadership.

There are no shortages of problems and opportunities. Leadership is not about telling others they ought to solve these problems. It's about seeing a problem and accepting personal responsibility for doing something about it. And it's about holding yourself accountable for the actions you take. The next time you see a problem and say "Why doesn't someone do something about this?" take a look in the mirror and say instead, "I'll be the someone to do something about it."

Testing Yourself

Effective change leadership begins with you. When you boil it all down, focused attention creates energy, and energy creates results.

Toward the end of Peter Drucker's seven decades of being perhaps the 20th century's greatest managerial thought-leader, he identified a single factor that united all great leaders: *their commitment.*

As a leader, for any change you're leading or race you're running, constantly ask yourself and those you lead how you rate on the following measures of commitment (Figure 7).

Calendar test	How much time are you spending on this initiative?

Energy test	How much passion and attention are you demonstrating?
Rhetoric test	How much time do you spend talking publically and privately about the change? Are you telling the story using both facts and emotion?
Resource test	How much money and talent are you directing toward the change?
Relationship test	How much effort are you putting in to work with others across all disciplines related to this change?

Figure 7. Testing your actions for perceived effectiveness regarding specific change initiatives

On a scale of 0-10, where 0 is "none at all" and 10 is "going full out" in these categories related to change initiatives, where do you fall?

Remember, the ability to effect beneficial change is the hallmark of an effective leader. Keep asking yourself and those you lead where you fall on the 0-10 scale—either regarding your leadership in general or on specific initiatives. Are you trending upward in your commitment?

To go full out, you'll need to mitigate risks—the subject of Part Four.

PART FOUR

Mitigating Risk

Chapter 12 / Assessing Risk and Consequences

AS WE'VE ALREADY DISCUSSED, while change is critically important to business and personal success, it's also fraught with risk. Therefore, as a leader it's your responsibility to tread softly along that delicate line between the potential dangers and anticipated rewards of any initiative you may lead.

In any endeavor, it's possible that the rewards simply don't justify the risks required to achieve them. Whether that risk is financial, legal, ethical, or of some other nature, you need to rationally weigh all the contributing factors before you charge up that hill, particularly if the stakes are large.

But, there are times when even the best-laid plans fail miserably. When that happens, you need to do your best not only to minimize the damage, but also to take the time to learn as much as possible from the failure, so that it doesn't happen again. Let me tell you a story about just that.

My Unfortunate—but Valuable—Cup Car Incident

This personal—and quite literally impactful—experience illustrates the idea that it's the little things that matter.

So much of what we do in life has little effect at first, but the results of our decisions and our actions accumulate, both good and bad. The trick is being able to catch and correct the bad things before they get out of control, but sometimes that's hard to do. The longer you let things go before correcting, the harder it is to get them back under control. Whether it's driving, leading, or almost anything else in life, being able to make the right corrections early is as much art as it is science—an art at which I failed miserably and rather publicly while driving a Porsche 911 racing car *much* too fast.

But I'm getting ahead of myself.

It happened at the Porsche Sport Driving School. I was one of just six students taking part in the school's *911 GT3 Cup Car Experience*, the highest-level course they offer. To qualify, I'd already been through the rest of their full complement of courses, as had all the other students. So there we were: six instructors, six students, and two full days with the school's best, fastest, and most expensive cars at Barber Motorsports Park in Birmingham, Alabama, one of the most beautiful race tracks in the world.

It was a gearhead's dream come true.

The first day, we drove street cars. Starting with regular street 911s we quickly moved up to 911 GT3s. The GT3 is basically a street-legal racing car, so it's fast, but still at least a little civilized. Both of these cars were terrific fun but they were just the warm-up. The appetizers, as it were.

It was the second day that was the big deal. That's when we were going to drive the Cup Cars. These are full-on, factory-built racing cars. They're fast and unforgiving and Porsche only makes enough of them to sell to bona fide racing teams, so you have to be known to the factory to even have a chance of buying one.

Needless to say, I was really looking forward to finally getting a chance to drive an actual Porsche factory racing car. In retrospect, maybe I was looking forward to it a little too much.

It was the second day, toward the end of the morning when it happened, but the first day hadn't been all that great for me, despite the wonderful cars and venue. I hadn't been there all the way, mentally. Business issues and other concerns kept me from fully concentrating on my driving, and I hadn't slept well either.

Because of my so-so performance that first day, I really wanted to prove something to myself—and probably the instructors, too—on the second day, so I was trying awfully hard.

And, just to get everything out on the table, I had a distraction. Really, in the grand scheme of things, it was such a small matter that it's hardly worth mentioning, but when I arrived at the track that second morning, the helmet I'd used the day before was gone. Not a big deal. I found a replacement, but for some reason the visor on the new helmet wouldn't stay up. I prefer to drive closed cars with my visor up, so I should have just gone looking for another helmet with a visor that worked properly. But I didn't. I kept the bad one.

Looking back, I realize I wasn't fully in the moment that second day, either, even though at the time I thought I was fine. I was still tired, and my thoughts were partially focused on issues outside the track. Add to that the distraction of having to fiddle with the darned visor several times a lap and, with all of that going on, I really wasn't concentrating hard enough on the one thing that actually mattered at the moment, which was my driving.

I know that now.

Probably because I felt like I had something to prove, and because I had let my ego start making decisions on my behalf, I was working overly hard in the first few laps to build up speed. I wanted to go too fast, too soon.

I was pushing my own limits awfully hard but, in addition to all my other distractions, the car itself was a bit overwhelming. It was just *so different.*

The Porsche 911 Cup is all race car, which means it is *very* loud, *very* fast, and that it does *exactly* what you tell it to do, *right now*, with no filters or safety nets. This is a car for experts. Unlike the street cars we'd driven the day before, the Cup Car doesn't have stability control or traction control, or any of the many other little electronic nannies that silently help out when you do something stupid on the street. Compared to the street 911 or even the GT3, the Cup Car was brutal, hyper-responsive, and I was pushing it pretty hard.

Looking back, I was at the upper end of my personal *stretch* zone as I tried to bend that bucking thoroughbred to my will. Its capabilities were certainly greater than mine, but I was trying very hard to push myself out near the car's limits.

Turn four at Barber comes at the top of a steep uphill climb. You can't see over the top, making it a very fast, blind turn. When you're carrying a lot of speed, it's a turn you absolutely *have* to get right because there is very little room for error. On my fourth lap, I missed the apex by three feet, which doesn't sound like a lot, but at full speed it is *much* too much.

As I tried to correct, the tail of the car started to slide.

My instructor, a highly experienced racer, immediately yelled *"Brake! Brake! Brake!"* into the intercom but I thought I'd caught it so I ignored him and gave it more gas; which is when things went from *bad* to *worse*. With the tail already sliding, adding more throttle transformed our slide into a full-out spin and the car pirouetted across the track and out into the grass, completely and entirely out of control.

According to the telemetry, we were doing 105 miles per hour when all this started. In a fraction of a second I went from being fully in control to being a helpless passenger in a spinning projectile. Brakes, steering—nothing had any effect and, worse, I had taken somebody along with me. In what seemed like slow motion, we slowly spun 180 degrees while sliding 200 yards across the track and through the infield before slamming into a guardrail and crushing the instructor's side of the car. At the moment of impact, we were still doing 55 miles per hour.

I'd crashed the Cup Car.

Hard.

It was a big hit and, worse, it was all my fault. The car was totaled and my ribs hurt like hell. No matter what my distraction factors may have been, ultimately it was me who'd lost control, who hadn't adequately recognized and reacted to the risks. It was me who'd screwed it up.

Period.

Fortunately, my instructor and I weren't seriously hurt—shaken for sure, with weeks of sore ribs ahead, but we were basically okay. But here's the thing: even though my ribs were hurting badly and I'd just destroyed a wonderful car, I didn't simply sulk off mumbling, "Darn, I crashed it." Not that I was happy about it, mind you—but I recognized that this was a learning moment for me.

The damage was already done. I'd gone from *stretch* into *panic* and then well beyond that. Nothing I could do would undo anything that had happened up until that point, but what I *could* do was try to get as much value as I could from the experience—to learn from my screw-up. I thought about my friend Jean Pavilliard, an Everest-accomplished climber, who once remarked, "It's not about how well you climb, it's about how well you climb back."

Hurley Haywood was on the track that day and upon returning to the pits, came up to me, shook his head, and teased, "So, did you run out of talent at the top of the hill?"

Clearly, I had.

At lunch, Cass Whitehead asked if I minded him using my crash video as a learning aid for the other students. Although it was embarrassing to be used as that kind of example, I saw this as positive. Hopefully, the others could benefit from my mistake, salvaging some good from what had happened, and maybe I would learn something, too.

I sat quietly in the back of the room while Cass reviewed the video in excruciating detail. From his analysis, I saw both why and how it had all happened.

Over and over again.

Through the afternoon, I had a chance to talk to most of the instructors, all of whom said they'd experienced a similar incident at one time or another. I asked, "What do you do about that when it happens?"

They each said essentially the same thing: "You've got to get past it, but first you want to understand exactly what happened."

Of course I knew that in this risky environment bad things could happen. The trick was to understand my part in it. So for many days afterward, I turned it and churned it and worked the whole thing over in my head.

It wasn't until a week or two later, with my ribs still aching, that I realized my experience in the Cup Car was no different than anything else we do in business or otherwise.

Things can go wrong. They can rattle our beliefs about ourselves. We get fired, or don't get the promotion, or really miss our numbers. We totally screw up with a major customer, violate a political rule, or offend the native culture by not knowing what we're supposed to do. I've seen all of those situations from time to time with various executives I've coached.

As I've said, the unfortunate but brilliant function of pain is to get our attention. As often as not, it's our pains, our misses, and our mistakes that cause us to think the most deeply about how we might do things differently.

The better performers really take mistakes and setbacks to heart. They want to figure them out, to get in there to understand exactly what went wrong and why.

While I'd certainly spun off tracks in the past—with the attendant squealing tires and clouds of dust—my mistakes had resulted in little of consequence. Nothing in my history could hold a candle to crashing the Cup Car. That was a baptism of sorts, and it made me think about things differently.

It reminded me of a night some years earlier when I had the chance to meet Lieutenant Colonel Hal Moore. Hal is the real-life character on whom the movie *We Were Soldiers*, in which he was played by Mel Gibson, was based. The movie tells the story of the Battle of the Ia Drang Valley, the first major battle of the Vietnam War, fought between the U.S. and Vietnamese regulars. Hal was a West Point graduate and had served in Korea. He was tasked in the 1950s with helping the Army determine what it could do with the combination of helicopters and infantry in the then newly created armored air cavalry.

His force of specially trained fighters landed in an area that turned out to be the home of a significantly larger force of Viet Cong, and there ensued a horrific and historic battle.

This confrontation has been studied many times over the years, and the U.S.'s victory was in no small part credited to Hal's remarkable leadership and commitment to his men. Of course, like all battles, the first skirmish didn't decide it. It was the second and third encounters—where we would attack them, then they would attack us back—that some of the most brutal fighting occurred.

The story is legend, and I remember having a great evening talking to Hal. I'd seen the movie and knew a bit of the rest of the story, but what I really wanted to know was, *how did it change his life?*

He was 84 when I met him. One of the things he told me was this: "Every time I'm ready to make a decision, right before I finalize it, I always try to stop and ask myself, 'What else am I not thinking about? What else am I not considering?' Even after I think I've made the decision."

Since I had the Cup Car incident, I hear Hal Moore's voice asking, "What else am I not thinking about?" It has changed my approach to high-performance driving and how I assess risk, both on the track and otherwise.

For instance, last fall—before the Cup Car incident—I took my street car, a significantly modified, turbocharged Miata, to High Plains Raceway and drove at relatively high speeds on the track. Although the car has roll hoops, it doesn't have a full cage. Not even a full roll bar. Since the accident occurred, I've been taking a mental inventory of possible downsides. In retrospect, I realized I wasn't correctly assessing the potential risk. Although it's highly unlikely that car would ever flip over, it could; and if it did, it's not set up with adequate protection. In other words, if that admittedly low-percentage situation *did* happen, it could kill me.

That's a big downside.

I have a second Miata that's set up as a race car. It has a full cage and all the proper safety gear, but it's a lot more work to get to the track. First, I have to get the truck and the trailer, then load and unload the car at both ends of the trip. Because it's not street legal and I can't drive it to the gas station, so I have to carry extra fuel. I also have to bring tools and spare parts, two sets of tires, and even a change of clothes. Taking the race car was a big effort, particularly for relatively small amounts of track time, so as often as not, I'd leave it at home and take the street car because it was so much easier to do.

But not anymore. Not since my crash and subsequent reevaluation of risk. I take the race car now, despite the extra work, because the risk/reward calculation is so much more in my favor.

Both my accident and my time with Hal Moore gave me a deeper respect for the value of considering all the alternate possibilities. Although there's more to it, I believe that's also how our better executives and leaders develop. Every leader crashes once in a while. Those wrecks can come in the form of missed objectives, hiring mistakes, or bad acquisitions.

So, the question of performance isn't whether or not you ever crash. You're *going* to crash sometimes. Even the greatest racing drivers do. The measure of your abilities is in how you recover and learn from these events. It's your reaction to what goes wrong that ultimately determines your upper limit as a driver and as a leader.

Chapter 13 / Situational Awareness

IN RE-RE-*RE*-REVIEWING MY CRASH in the Cup Car and my mental state at the time, I realized that I was lacking a sufficient degree of what is known as *situational awareness*.

Situational awareness, or *SA* as it's often called, is a critical skill for doing anything at an extraordinary level of competence. Whether that's driving a racing car, running an organization, or performing virtually any other complex task that requires quick decision-making, SA is a core component of consistent success.

The concept of SA was first developed by the U.S. Air Force during the Korean War as part of an effort to understand what made certain pilots much better than others in the heat of battle. Researchers discovered that these high performers all shared a heightened sense of the environment around them. They instinctively understood how the elements of that environment could be combined with their own actions to impact and shape conditions in the immediate future. Because their awareness was so finely tuned and constantly at work, these individuals had an extraordinary ability to respond to hazards and threats *as they emerged*. It seemed as if they could anticipate these conditions rather than having to react to them after they appeared.

Situational awareness is what was missing from my time in the Cup Car. I was *reacting*, not *anticipating*, and eventually it bit me. I was *behind* what was happening, not *ahead* of it.

This form of heightened SA quickly became known throughout the Air Force as "the ace factor." Subsequently, it's been studied and applied in all branches of the military, in commercial aviation, in health care, and by engineers who work to minimize systemic accidents.

Individuals with high SA are now defined as having *enhanced knowledge about the inputs and outputs of a particular system*. That is, they possess an innate feel for how the combination of circumstances, people, and events are likely to play out. They also clearly understand which of the many variables in any situation they're able to control.

Inadequate situational awareness is recognized as one of the key factors in accidents attributable to human error. Today, it's considered an essential skill in occupations in which information flow is high and poor decisions have serious consequences, such as piloting a plane, being on the front line in a war, and treating the critically ill.

The Scientific Definition of SA

Scientists who study SA note that it represents a balanced state of awareness, a midpoint between hyper-vigilance and complacency. It's an inherently relaxed state that puts little stress on the system and, because it's not tiring, can be sustained over long periods of time. People with high SA are able to enjoy the moment while simultaneously paying attention to the other things going on around them.

Not surprisingly, people with high situational awareness are also intensely present and alive in the moment—but not so absorbed that they aren't capable of making decisive moves. High SA correlates with being physiologically coherent and in one's "zone"—that area of relaxed concentration famously experienced by athletes, musicians, and others— while low SA correlates with being distracted, anxious, and more closed down mentally.

If you go back to two of my driving stories in this book, you can see the difference situational awareness makes. In that first ride I took with an instructor, he was not only driving flat-out but chatting amiably at the same time. He was calm, relaxed, and totally in the moment—demonstrating a high level of situational awareness.

In contrast, consider my experience in the Cup Car. I had other things on my mind and was distracted by the noise, the speed, and even the flopping visor on my helmet. I was clearly *not* in the moment, regardless of how much I may have wanted to be. That performance evidenced low situational awareness, and its outcome was not only poor, but it was dangerous.

Three Requirements for SA

High-functioning situational awareness requires three things. First, your mind needs to be relaxed and alert. Second, you need to be focused and relatively free of distractions. Finally, you need to be skilled in the fundamentals of the process in which you're engaging. In driving, that includes acceleration, braking, shifting gears, and steering, and may also include more advanced skills related to car control, racecraft, and a host of other topics. In business, it means having a strong understanding of the requirements of your role as well as the roles of those with whom you're working. There's always a lot to consider, and taking time to do so is part of being and acting like a professional.

A strong, almost innate, understanding of the fundamentals is critical to shortening the decision-making process. For instance, a study was recently done on the reaction times of racing drivers of various ages.[11] Not surprising, younger drivers have quicker reaction times, but that's not the whole story.

It turns out that younger drivers have quicker reaction times to *unknown stimuli,* or stimuli to which experience brings no value. For instance, pressing a button whenever you hear a particular sound or a flash of light. In that sort of situation, younger people have consistently better reaction times than older folks do.

But when you get out of the laboratory, the situation is different—because in the real world, experience counts. A key part of situational awareness is a finely tuned sense of what constitutes risk and a well-informed understanding of how conditions evolving around you might come together to constitute a threat.

It turns out that older drivers—which is to say, those with more driving experience—often react more quickly than younger ones *in real life* because they recognize familiar patterns. They can frequently anticipate the potential need for a reaction and, as a result, they're ready to react more appropriately, sooner.

Not only does this situational awareness more than level the playing field, it facilitates making smaller corrections sooner, which is a great deal less upsetting to the system as a whole.

My first driving instructor possessed uncanny smoothness at the controls because of his situational awareness. This ability includes pattern recognition, a skill and practice addressed in the next chapter that's highly useful both on the track and when leading in business.

Regaining Situational Awareness When Distracted

Here's a simple and highly useful way to re-establish your own situational awareness (sometimes referred to as mindfulness):

Take a deep breath, in and out. Pause, and then *look around.* Concentrate on the small details of everything within view. The leaves on the trees, the mail on your desk, the font on the dials on the dashboard.

Take another breath, in and out. Pause again, and *listen*—to the tick of the clock, the breath of the ventilation system, the birds outside, the traffic.

Take a third deep breath, pause once more, and *feel* your physical sensations—in your hands, in your body. Feel the chair, your clothes where they touch your skin, or the wheel in your hands.

And then move on.

This can be done anytime, in any place, and under nearly any conditions. It helps you quickly reconnect and reset yourself to "right here, right now."

Chapter 14 / Pattern Recognition

RECOGNIZING PATTERNS is a key part of situational awareness, which involves seeing the bigger picture in what you are doing as well as in what those around you are doing. For instance, as a racer, the behavior of the other drivers falls into recognizable patterns.

Patterns simplify our thinking because that which is familiar requires less thought to process than something new. This comes back to the idea of establishing neural connections in our brains. Pattern recognition is a big part of what moves us along the continuum from *panic* to *stretch* to *comfort*. Pattern recognition makes it vastly easier for us to deal with the masses of information bombarding us all day long, and it also makes it much easier to identify the outliers. Human brains are amazingly good at both recognizing patterns and recognizing the aberrations in patterns—if we pay attention.

Making Money with Pattern Recognition

In 2005—nearly three years before the U.S. housing bubble burst—John Paulson, founder and principal of the hedge fund Paulson & Co., sensed that something was wrong with the market. He suspected the roaring enthusiasm and runaway success that was being enjoyed by nearly everyone couldn't continue.

As chronicled by *The Wall Street Journal*, January 15, 2008:

> *"Like many legendary market killings . . . Mr. Paulson's sprang from defying conventional wisdom. In early 2006, the wisdom was that while loose lending*

standards might be of some concern, deep trouble in the housing and mortgage markets was unlikely. A lot of big Wall Street players were in this camp, as seen by the giant mortgage-market losses they're disclosing.

"'Most people told us house prices never go down on a national level, and that there had never been a default of an investment-grade-rated mortgage bond,' Mr. Paulson says. 'Mortgage experts were too caught up' in the housing boom."[12]

Paulson did several things right. First, he recognized the aberration in the stock market pattern, which later came to be known as "irrational exuberance." That was pattern recognition, and he wasn't the only person to see the potential problems at the time.

Second, he avoided target fixation. Most other fund managers were so caught up in making money that they never took the time to look far enough ahead to see the crash coming.

Ultimately, according to *The Telegraph*, the part of the bubble he and his team decided to bet against was the U.S. housing market. It was a bet that netted the firm $15 billion, with Paulson personally earning $3-4 billion in fees.[13]

When our brains process known patterns, the things that stand out become the signal and all the rest is treated as noise. We're filtering all the time, working though what's meaningful, what's not, and what can be ignored. John Paulson consciously used this often subconscious human capability to become one of the wealthiest people in the world.

The Importance of Experience in Developing Patterns

As mentioned earlier, Malcolm Gladwell states that success is largely the result of roughly 10,000 hours of practicing tasks specific to your particular field. I would suggest that a great deal of that value comes from having had enough time and experience to create the necessary patterns inside your head, available for recognition later.

The catch is, you can't simply depend on this information without question. You need to always be aware that the patterns you have and trust aren't infallible. They aren't 100 percent. I had a pattern in my head, all those years ago when I first drove on a race track, about how fast it was possible to drive a car. I was sure it was right, that it was a valid pattern, but as it turned out, I wasn't even *close* to being right.

In my crash with the Cup Car, I had underdeveloped pattern recognition for the environment and speed in which I was operating. My instructor was yelling for me to brake because *he* knew exactly what patterns were at work. My less-developed pattern for that situation said *give it some gas* and, well, you know how that ended.

Recognizing Patterns in a Business

In business, many of the cues, or patterns, used to determine how closely the organization is running to the limit of its capabilities are a great deal more subtle, albeit no less important, than those on a racetrack. So, how do you know how close you are to your upper limit in business? And, how do you know whether the limit you're pushing is your own personal limit or the business's *actual* limit?

Many different models are available for assessing the performance of a business. However, after literally hundreds of client engagements, Pilot Consulting developed a way of looking at organizations that quickly cuts through the complexity. It gets to the heart of what drives performance in most organizations.

We call our model the *Competitive Business Model*. It evolved during a time when I was regularly speaking to boards of directors and companies around the globe about the answer to the question, *Why is GE so good?* I needed a way to effectively illustrate the core components of the company's approach, and this model did the trick.

While this framework is based on a particularly GE-centric piece of research, it was derived from looking across all of GE's businesses. The resulting model has proven to be remarkably effective and accurate for assessing nearly every organization I've worked with over the past 20 years since we first figured it out.

As illustrated in Figure 8, the Competitive Business Model (CBM) has four quadrants, and we've found them to be absolutely essential to successfully running a consistently-competitive organization of any kind.

The model delivers actionable performance-improvement target areas in a way that's easily understandable and can be quickly evaluated in relation to any particular organization.

Competitive Business Model

Market-Based Vision & Strategy	Customer-Valued Metrics
Vision of competitive success	Identified customer satisfiers
Strategy of differentiation	Alignment with internal metrics
Grounding in customer needs/wants	Targets exceeding customer needs
Adaptive-Learning Culture	**Ongoing Process Innovation**
Act-learn-change discipline	Mapped & measured core processes
Skilled and empowering leaders	Stretch targets
Competent & committed workforce	Status quo challenged by process teams
Cross-boundary partnering	Quick response / empowerment by leaders

Figure 8: Pilot Consulting's Competitive Business Model

This framework guides us to recognize patterns of behavior and practices that explain and help predict performance gains or losses. By focusing on each of these four discrete areas—how well they are each being performed and how congruently they are being correlated—we get strong signals about the sort of corrective actions that may need to be taken.

Let's look at each quadrant in more detail.

1. *Market-Based Vision and Strategy*

This quadrant is about defining the realities of the business.

Given the talent you have and the capabilities of your team, what are you trying to achieve? Do you have a vision for achieving success that can be shared with and embraced by the organization? How are your products or services different from those of your competitors? Without differentiation, your product becomes a commodity and enters a market where price becomes the only viable strategy for standing out.

Given one or more discernible differences between your product(s) and those of your competitors, you have something unique to sell, making it possible to change the game in your favor. When your products, services, and experiences are unique, or have unique characteristics, they offer your customers more value, putting you in a position to charge a premium.

But all the differentiation in the world will do you no good if the products you make or the services you offer are unneeded or unwanted by your customers. Product strategy must always be based on satisfying actual client wants and/or needs.

2. *Customer-Valued Metrics*

Once you have a vision and a strategy, you move into the second quadrant, Customer-Valued Metrics, shown in the upper right corner of the model. Success over time requires metrics, or numbers against which you can measure the ongoing performance of the organization. Without some form of meaningful metrics, how can you know your level of performance? On the track, racers measure lap times, of course, but they measure a lot more than that. Cornering speed, brake pressure, and steering angle. Brake and tire temperatures. Oil pressure. All of these give critical insight into the performance of both the car and its driver and provide immediate feedback, which can be used to improve the performance of either or both.

In business, metrics include basics such as financial statements, but what matters even more to the long-term success of the organization is *whatever matters to its customers.* Therefore, your organization needs to focus on metrics that relate to things that matter to your customers. While profit is important to track and know, profit is the result of and a reward for doing things right. It's not the purpose of the organization, nor is it of much interest to your customers.

Customers are more interested in product quality, availability, and/or innovation. How does what you provide feel, or work, or taste? Does it make your customers happier, smarter, or more successful?

In many companies, the voice of the customer is thought to be inherent because, after all, what the company produces is what its customers are buying. But translating that inherent value into meaningful internal metrics raises the game to a whole new level. One in which the value of the product is not just theoretical.

It's your job as the leader to find ways to understand the characteristics of your offerings that make them attractive and satisfying to your customers. Then you need to define and build internal measurement systems aligned with these characteristics. You measure the things that matter to your customers and set goals that push the organization to over-achieve on customer expectations. This concentration on over-satisfying customer wants and needs will ultimately drive profitability and sustainable business.

3. Ongoing Process Innovation

Related to creating metrics based on customer values is Ongoing Process Innovation, shown in the lower right quadrant of this framework. The idea of ongoing process innovation speaks to the heart of value delivery. It's about establishing and maintaining a mindset focused on continuously improving your company's products and services and their delivery.

This starts with the customer-valued metrics identified in quadrant 2, using them to push to the next level by setting stretch targets. In includes empowering teams charged with challenging the status quo and involves leaders who are open to change and can quickly respond as required.

By engaging the entire organization, challenging current processes and beliefs, and building the idea of improvement into the very fabric of the business, you develop a company that's ready and able to continuously transform itself in meaningful ways.

4. Adaptive Learning Culture

Last, but no less important, is developing an Adaptive Learning Culture, shown in the bottom left quadrant. This is the final piece of the puzzle that pulls all the other pieces together.

An Adaptive Learning Culture has a built-in reflection process that gains insight by asking not only *What are our best practices?* but also *What are our worst practices?* We've consistently found this core value of reflection to be inherent in top performers that have proven themselves able to deliver sustainable performance over the long haul.

The disciplines and related skills shown in all of the quadrants of the Competitive Business Model aren't static. Rather, they define a continuum of action. Develop products or services your customers want to buy. Measure what you do in terms that are meaningful to those customers. Find ways to innovate and improve what you do. And, finally, make it possible for your people and your partners to learn and grow. To mature. To see ahead and, from that, to develop the next product or service, beginning the cycle of business life anew.

Think about adapting and creating a market-based vision and strategy— one that's continuously in motion and adapting to ever-changing conditions. This fourth critical area identifies how capable any given company, team, or leader is. Do they all continuously ask the questions needed to drive change? Are they working with and through their people to go beyond what exists today?

Focusing on the disciplines in all four quadrants and the relationships between them can quickly help you recognize and understand patterns of behavior, current capabilities, and the relative health and vitality of your enterprise.

Chapter 15 / It's Less About You, It's More About Them, and It's Definitely About Us

MANY OF THE COMPARISONS made in this book have been between the business executive and the racing driver, an analogy that works because, in both cases, we're talking about individuals. But when we start thinking about organizations, the better comparison is often to the racing *team*. After all, the team, or department, or organization is not just one person; it's a group of people working together toward achieving shared, challenging goals.

In any but the shortest of races, success on the track requires not only a fast car and a skilled driver but also an experienced pit crew, trained mechanics, team managers, engineers, and even strategists to make it all work. No matter how great a job the driver does, if any one of those people makes even a small mistake, the success of the entire team is threatened. Nowhere is that more true than in endurance racing, where races can last 6, 12, or even 24 hours.

In the most successful racing teams, every member knows exactly what he or she is expected to do and has practiced it endlessly, along with multiple contingencies for when things go wrong. They've developed sets of patterns and behaviors that make it easier to react quickly and correctly to the actual events occurring around them. That's not so different from the world of business.

Today, we compete in a global environment where unanticipated threats and business uncertainties are the only things we can count on. The military refers to common patterns seen in environments in which they serve by the acronym VUCA, which stands for volatile, uncertain, complex, and ambiguous. And, much like a team in the middle of a 24-hour race, we need to be able to continually adjust our strategies and plans to meet developing situations and temper those adjustments in light of the larger objective. The quick reactions and flexible adaptability needed to maximize short-term opportunities have to be balanced with the need to survive—and better yet *thrive*—for the duration.

Pattern recognition can be incredibly valuable in this regard. By understanding and recognizing the patterns of her business, the effective CEO can keep her fingers on the pulse of the organization even though she can't be party to all the details.

Silo Wars

Leaders have to be especially vigilant in larger organizations where individual teams or departments can become "siloed." That is, they can become so insulated from the actions and decisions of other related departments that they're no longer focused on the broader common goal.

For instance, there's very often a natural conflict between Engineering and Purchasing. Engineering wants the best materials and tightest specifications, and they want them regardless of cost. Purchasing, on the other hand, cares most about cost, availability, and reliability of the vendor, so it's natural that these two groups conflict from time to time. But if that discord is left to fester and grow, if barriers are allowed to remain, and if there's no communication or cross-pollination between the groups, it's almost impossible to come to the best solutions for the business as a whole.

It's the role of leadership to break through these barriers and bring the teams together under a common understanding of the broader overall vision and the mission being served. That way, the internal silos don't end up winning the battles while the company loses the war.

A recent, quite public example of such a silo war is the GM ignition switch debacle. By most accounts, this was a matter of, first, a lower-level engineer not being given a voice; second, higher-ups making uninformed decisions; and, finally, a lot of other people not challenging that decision because it wasn't their job. It wasn't a function of their silo.

By making these decisions, GM saved what was reported by the *New York Daily News* to be $0.57 per vehicle.[14] However, as of December 2014, the company had been forced to commit more than $2 billion to the recall, to say nothing of the 42 deaths attributed to the faulty switch.

What should have been an easy decision and an equally easy fix was never implemented because one group of people said *cost is all that matters,* while others said, in effect, *it's not my job.*

This is an unfortunate but excellent example of what you see when you have fragmentation or "silofication" of effort buried inside a large and complex bureaucracy.

So a leader can't be a lone ranger. Everyone in the organization needs to pull together and cooperate for the success of all—and the leader's job is to facilitate this cooperation.

Chapter 16 / The Final Lap

WHETHER IT'S DRIVING YOUR CAR to dinner, or leading a team on a project at work, every day there are times when you're "behind the wheel" and "driving" toward your next destination. Think of these times as opportunities for personal development, to do whatever it is you're doing a little bit better.

If you're in the car and driving, *better* means a smoother, safer ride, with your eyes focused far ahead. At work, the challenges are different, but no less definable. In both cases, the goal is to be better today than you were yesterday, and better again tomorrow.

Business and racing both move through cycles. Whether it's laps around the track or the product life cycle of design, development, introduction, and maintenance, it's important to follow these cycles—to do your laps—with consistent disciplines. Find what works for you by knowing the cycle you are in and anticipating the cycle, or cycles, ahead.

Your overall process of growth will undoubtedly include a few failures and a lot of change, but as the following story proves, that's not necessarily a bad thing.

Growing, Failing, Learning, Changing

John Margaritis is an American success story. Born in Greece, he came to the U.S. for college, fell in love, married a girl from Ohio, and has been living in Connecticut for the past 25 years.

After earning his MBA, John helped start Pepsi's first bottled water division, then was part of the introduction of Slice, Lipton in a Can, and several other well-known products. Later, he started Lunchables for Oscar Mayer and helped Cadbury Schweppes acquire Dr. Pepper, 7-Up, and A&W before teaming up with Sara Lee to create the Wonderbra.

Eventually, John helped expand the reach of a then relatively unknown clothing designer named Tommy Hilfiger and made his fortune.

He explains: "I retired at forty with millions of dollars in the bank, but then ended up losing almost all of it when the .com bubble imploded. You know, they say you learn from failures not from successes, and that was definitely my case. That's when I decided to become an entrepreneur."

John started a company called the Ledgemoor Group, which has now launched more than 30 businesses and consults for many others.

"But I'd like to emphasize two things," he tells me. "The first is about failure. I believe you cannot become a better person unless you fail. Why? Because somehow, we seem to learn much faster and better from our failures than we do from our successes. In our culture we avoid failure. It's not what the American dream is all about, but the reality is that almost every success you see has emerged from some kind of a failure, or from a number of different failures. We have to embrace failure in order to have success.

"The second is that breakthroughs come from small changes. They come from the details. I see this over and over again, and I argue with some of my clients who say, 'We want a breakthrough idea here.' I tell them it's going to happen by focusing on the little things, on incremental changes to their current products or services.

He continued, "A good example is the Porsche 911. It's 50 years old but is still one of the best cars available. Why? Because Porsche's culture is such that it has been making small, incremental changes to the 911 throughout its entire history. They keep moving it forward."

Better and Better Wins the Race

This idea of always looking to achieve something *better* is not new. Even *slightly better* counts, as top performers will tell you. It's this spirit of continuous improvement—*the relentless everyday pursuit of better*—that builds new perceptions in others and capabilities in yourself that will eventually take you to a higher level on the track, in your career, and in how you live your life.

In this book, I've shared what I believe are fundamental insights into both the mindset and practices of top performers that, when applied consistently, can help you deliver better results more often. Whatever your next target, whatever your hoped-for goals, it's your everyday attitude and actions that will determine the odds of your next success.

Your ability to use good judgment and make smart decisions comes from experience, and experience comes from *seat time*. In driving terms, seat time comes from driving and from studying driving. In business leadership, seat time comes in the form of your day-to-day performance. Even if some of your most valuable experiences come as the result of poor decisions and bad judgment, always remember that it's the brilliant function of pain to get your attention.

Your focused attention creates energy. Routinely practicing the attitudes and skills described here until they become your standard operating procedures multiplies that energy. These efforts will positively and consistently lead you to better outcomes and help you win your race.

See you on the track.

Chris Cappy

"Keep your eyes on the road, keep your hands upon the whee 'el..."

—As heard on the radio and in driver ed

Appendix / Everyday-Driving Tips from Racing

FROM STUDYING PROFESSIONAL DRIVERS and by participating in high-performance drivers' education events, I've learned a number of small but significant changes we can all make in the way we handle our day-to-day driving. These changes will markedly improve our driving skills and make us safer, more relaxed, and better prepared to tackle the rest of the day.

I'd like to share these tips and hope you take them to heart. They involve a certain way of seeing, thinking, and feeling when driving.

Seeing

The biggest difference between the way top-level racers drive compared to the average driver is in how they use their eyes.

I mentioned target fixation earlier in the book: the unrelenting *over*-focus on one thing to the neglect of everything else around you. Unfortunately, this seems to describe the way most drivers on the road today use their eyes. They often focus on objects much too close ahead–– often the bumper of the car immediately in front of them, but sometimes just the road. Even on an empty highway, most drivers look only a few car lengths ahead.

It's best, however, to look as far down the road as you can see, and use your *peripheral vision* to see what's immediately to either side of you. You become aware of the edge of the road, other vehicles alongside you, parked cars, pedestrians, and so on. This may seem strange, and if you've never driven that way, you may find it harder to do at first than you think, but by doing nothing other than raising your eyes to look farther down the road, you will vastly improve the quality of your driving.

Here's why:

First, by looking farther down the road, you can anticipate actions you'll have to take much sooner than if you're focused nearby. You may see an upcoming curve, debris in the road, or cars ahead slamming on their brakes. Whatever you see, you can prepare for it and react more appropriately with less or no panic.

Second, by looking farther down the road, your use of the steering wheel and pedals will naturally become more fluid. Perhaps you've ridden with someone who constantly jerks the car back and forth with the wheel or jumps on and off the brakes and gas in reaction to minor changes in traffic flow. Chances are pretty good that person was fixated only on the car ahead.

By being aware of the road and where it goes, you can much more easily make small steering corrections to keep yourself on course. Ironically, it's easier to know where you are on the road when you're looking at cars a quarter of a mile ahead than it is if you're looking at the road a car length or two in front of you.

Similarly, if you can see the whole line of cars ahead and not just the one that's *immediately* ahead, you can anticipate the need to brake or accelerate much sooner and more efficiently than you would otherwise.

So, the most important thing to do to improve your driving is to *look farther ahead*.

Thinking

The next most important thing racing drivers and the best drivers on the street do involves the way they *think*. That is, how they understand what's going on around them and how they anticipate what they'll need to do next.

On the track, that might be anticipating what the drivers around you are likely to do and what your response might be. For instance, let's say you're headed down a long straight into a heavy braking zone—an ideal place to pass—while being dogged from behind by a close competitor. You can anticipate he'll likely try to move to the inside to get past you under braking. Thus, you may decide to move toward the inside early on, forcing your competitor to make his passing attempt around the longer outside of the turn, which is harder to do successfully.

Of course, on the street your anticipation is about different things. It's about kids who might jump out from between parked cars, cars pulling out unexpectedly, doors opening into your path from parked cars, or any number of other possibilities. You can anticipate some of these by seeing them begin to happen—early, of course, because you're looking far ahead. Others you can anticipate from a combination of seeing what's around you and considering what might happen far enough in advance to have a reaction plan.

So, *thinking* is the second most important skill of the best drivers.

Feeling

You've probably heard that the best racers have a feel for the car, and that's true. Through their hands and feet, their legs and seat, skilled drivers can quite literally feel what the car is doing. Those feelings let them know how much harder they can turn or brake as they approach the limit of what's possible.

And while I hope you don't approach your car's physical limits on the street, being able to feel what the car is doing as you drive is important to driving more skillfully. This starts with where you position the seat and how you hold the wheel.

When you're properly positioned in the car, you'll meet the following conditions:

- Your knees will be slightly bent, even with the pedals depressed all the way down to the floor.

- You'll be able to move your feet back and forth between the pedals without your knees getting in the way of turning the steering wheel.

- When sitting all the way back in the seat, you'll be able to extend your arm straight ahead and contact the top of the wheel somewhere in the area between your wrist and the base of your thumb.

Once you've met these conditions, it's time to adjust the mirrors so you can use all three of them without changing position, other than turning your head. No leaning forward or to the side. You want to be able to easily scan all of them with your back held firmly in place against the seat.

As you drive, hold the wheel lightly at the 3- and 9 o'clock positions. You were probably taught to use 10 and 2, which is also okay, but 3 and 9 give you the most leverage and the most control of the car.

As you use the pedals, use them gently. *Roll* on and off the gas pedal, then *squeeze* on and off the brakes. Pay attention to the people riding with you. When you're driving well, they won't be jerking back and forth in their seats. Play a game with yourself and see if you can drive so your passengers can't quite tell when you transition from throttle to brake.

A smooth and controlled ride is the goal here, whether on the track or the street. You'll most likely achieve this goal if you look far ahead, anticipate the actions you'll need to take, and feel what the car is doing. Following these three tips, your experience of driving will be both safer and more enjoyable.

Acknowledgments / "Pit Crew"

I now fully appreciate how the process of writing a book can take on a life of its own. From where it all started several years ago, with a little (and sometimes a lot) of help from my friends, this book has ended up in a far better place! I'd like to acknowledge a few main members of my "pit crew" in this endeavor:

First of all, thank you to Scott Good, who has been a terrific collaborator, pace setter, contributor, and coauthor. Although we made a decision somewhere along the way that it would be less confusing and therefore more valuable for readers to tell this story in the first-person as a single voice, this book is very much a team effort.

Scott was able to take my business and consulting experiences, combine them with his own, and then sprinkle in a deep understanding of racing and of driving to tell our combined story in way that's gratifyingly cohesive, compelling and, approachable even for those less obsessed with cars and racing than we are.

A special call out to Hurley Haywood for his time, generosity, support, and friendship.

Thanks to Porsche Sport Driving School (PSDS) team friends and coaches for the track—in particular, Jeff Purner, President, Jeff Purner & Associates and Manager, Porsche Sport Driving School.

Thanks, also, to the great team of professional racers and instructors at PSDS, who have helped me to be better: Cass Whitehead, Brian

Cunningham, John Lewis, Rich Hull, and Doc Bundy—and the many other contributors to remarkable PSDS experiences. To Bob Sanderson for his good words and those two cigarettes during my hour in need.

Special thanks to Daniel Eastman for his contributions and manuscript review and to Sally Helgesen for our initial work and her enthusiastic support.

Too numerous to mention are the driving enthusiasts/business leaders, and friends with whom I've been on the track, but a special call to Paul Kirincic, Jim Schoedinger, Ed Dowling, Darcy Marud, Chris Riopelle, Cheryl Smith, John Marguritis, Darrin Rohr, and Wellborn Jack. Special call also to Tom Falk for his edits and track time. You have each played an important part in the process.

My gratitude also goes to:

The Skip Barber Racing School for training.

Walter Irvine for his review and comments, perhaps the most important of which pointing us to the idea of using the friction circle as a metaphor for much more than just driving. Thanks to Julie Soltis for her input, as well.

US Air's David Palmer for his instructional information on pilot training and human factors.

The crew at Flyin' Miata & Red Rock Racers: Bill and Teri Cardell, Keith Tanner, Jeremy Ferber, and Brandon Fitch. Also their racing-track buddies and instructors Goodloe Suttler and Shannon McMaster. You have all helped keep the machines running.

My Learning Network friends and accomplished authors who have inspired and supported this project with their time and coaching: Jim Kouzes, Joel Barker, Marshall Goldsmith, Richard Leider, John Alexander, Mark Levy, and Beverly Kaye. Larry Lyons for his prodding encouragement (in memory of our mentor Richard Beckhard).

Thanks also to other colleagues and collaborators:

David Giber for initiating this work with me and for his ongoing support throughout.

Jon Tandler for his friendship and legal perspective.

Dr. Joe Dispenza for his insights on brain research and habit formation.

Myron Radio for his review and perspective.

Jake Breeden for his support and reviews.

Bo Stambaugh for his encouragement and review. Bo, you are sadly missed.

Mark Chimsky for his professional editing support.

The Harvard Business Review for rejecting the concept, further motivating me to bring it to life.

Lastly, to my wife Andrea, with more appreciation than can ever be conveyed in print for your full support through all the ups and downs, twists and turns in life and with this little book too. You have had my back all the way. You inspire me to be better every day.

About the Author / **Chris Cappy**

CHRIS CAPPY FOUNDED PILOT CONSULTING CORPORATION in 1995 as a firm specializing in leadership development, action learning, and implementation of strategic objectives for corporations in the Americas, Europe, and Asia Pacific regions. Today, the Pilot network includes more than 40 senior consultants, thought leaders, and training specialists with extensive global experience.

Chris has more than 30 years of consulting and training experience in the areas of business strategy formulation, change management design and execution, executive/team coaching, and leadership education.

For four years, he worked with the award-winning Executive Challenge Program at Boston University's School of Management, an innovator in experiential and action learning methodologies. For 11 years, he was a faculty member at General Electric's Crotonville and served as a lead consultant with Workout for GE Appliances.

Between 1995 and 2001, he and the Pilot team acted as the sole global provider for the design and implementation of IBM's Accelerate Change Together initiative, running hundreds of ACT sessions in over 25 countries and considered integral to IBM's transformation in the 1990s.

Chris is a member of The Learning Network, a consortium of business writers, consultants, and innovators in the leadership development space, and has published articles on the topics of leading accelerated change and action learning.

He holds a B.S. in Production Management from Rochester Institute of Technology. He's also a graduate of Boston University's Management Development Program and of Columbia University's Advanced Organizational Development Program, and holds numerous other certifications.

Chris is based in Colorado with his wife Andrea and son Allen Joseph.

About the Author / Scott Good

SCOTT GOOD IS AN ENTHUSIASTIC INNOVATOR with more than 35 years of business leadership experience. A serial entrepreneur, he has broad experience in a wide range of industries including manufacturing, graphic arts, publishing, and software.

His experience and skills make him uniquely able to cut through conflicting requirements to uncover innovative and often unexpected solutions for clients which have included: Abbott Laboratories, American Electric Power, Battelle Memorial Institute, Chrysler Financial, Comerica Bank, Honda Research & Development, IBM, Nationwide Insurance, the U.S. Department of Defense, and others.

Scott acted as chief architect and interface designer on three of the world's most innovative workflow management software products and has extensive experience with user interface/user experience design.

An avid writer and public speaker, Scott has published more than 70 articles on topics related to software, interface design, and automobile racing. Prior to his collaboration on *Driving Leaders,* he published a novel, *Loss of Control,* which revolves around the search for truth in the murder of an amateur racing driver.

Scott lives in Charlotte, North Carolina, with his wife and the youngest of his four children.

Endnotes

1 Duke Corporate Education "2013 CEO Study: Leading in Context."
   http://www.dukece.com/elements/docs/LeadingInContext.pdf

2 Ibid.

3 Marshall Pruett, *Racer* magazine online,
   http://www.racer.com/more/viewpoints/item/110547-pruett-inside-the-audi-f1-
   rumors, November 4, 2014.

4 From his keynote speech at the 48th Annual Center for Automotive Research
   Management Briefing Seminars, December 8, 2013.

5 Malcolm Gladwell, *Outliers: The Story of Success.* Back Bay Books: Reprint edition, 2011.

6 Charles Duhigg, *The Power of Habit: Why We Do What We Do in Life and Business.* Random
   House Trade Paperbacks: Reprint edition, 2014.

7 Arijit Chatterjee and Donald C. Hambrick, "It's All about Me: Narcissistic Chief
   Executive Officers and Their Effects on Company Strategy and Performance,"2006.
   http://mario.gsia.cmu.edu/micro_2009/chatterjee_hambrick_2007.pdf

8 Peter Manso, "What I'd Do Differently," *Car and Driver.* Hearst: May 2013.
   http://www.caranddriver.com/features/what-id-do-differently-roger-penske-feature

9 James M. Kouzes and Barry Z. Posner, *The Leadership Challenge: How to Make Extraordinary
   Things Happen in Organizations.* Jossey-Bass: 5th edition, 2012.

10 James M. Kouzes and Barry Z. Posner, *The Truth about Leadership: The No-Fads, Heart-of-the-
   Matter Facts You Need to Know.* Jossey-Bass: 1st edition, 2010.

11 Stephen Cox blog, SopwithMotorsports.com, *Racing Past 40, part II: Slower Reaction Times
   and other Famous Lies.*
   http://www.sopwithmotorsports.com/blog/short-track-racing/item/236-racing-past-40-
   part-ii-slower-reaction-times-and-other-famous-lies.html

12 Gregory Zuckerman, "Trader Made Billions on Subprime," *The Wall Street Journal.*
   January 15, 2008,
   http://www.wsj.com/news/articles/SB120036645057290423.

13 James Quinn, "John Paulson: the man who made billions betting on a US housing
   crash," *The Telegraph.* April 16, 2010.
   http://www.telegraph.co.uk/finance/newsbysector/banksandfinance/7599203/John-
   Paulson-the-man-who-made-billions-betting-on-a-US-housing-crash.html.

[14] The Associated Press, "Cost to fix faulty General Motors ignition switch behind 13 deaths was 57 cents: congress," *New York Daily News.* April 1, 2014.
http://www.nydailynews.com/news/national/cost-fix-faulty-gm-ignition-switch-57-cents-congress-article-1.1742342